AWAKEN TO
LIVING

"After having known Asttarte nearly 15 years now, I can say, unequivocally, that she is woman gifted with a purpose, mission, and vision, to open the hearts of men and women, and to stay open regardless of the pain or consequences. If there were ever a path to be created in Tantra to commit to Love, no matter what the cost, Asttarte is certainly one of its most dedicated pioneers. Her book, *Awaken to Living: Tantra for Your Whole Life*, is a living testament to her Goddess given purpose and mission in life to deliver this message."
- Richard Anton Diaz, founder of Sexy Spirits

"*Awaken to Living; Tantra for Your Whole Life*" is the perfect treat for lovers of the body mind heart & soul connection. Asttarte's insightful, witty and relatable words have not only reaffirmed but also broadened my perspectives on intimacy and passion. I particularly appreciate her teachings on balance and transformation. With openness, spirit and healing this book motivates us to live life to its fullest potential; it is more than a good read, it is a manual for deeper fuller living. It's about understanding the needs and desires of the self, energy interplay, connectivity, sensuality, and then evolving these principles toward developing richer more meaningful intimate relationships with the self and those we love. Here we clearly realize that Tantra is not a practice, it's a lifestyle. I highly recommend this profound compilation of life essays for couples and individuals alike, for those who are curious about Tantra, as well as for those already practicing Tantric principles; but not only for reading and pondering, instead I urge you to take it further - experiment, practice, adopt and journal the results of the exercises, strategies and lifestyle it offers. I am blessed to know Asttarte in person, she truly is a rising star, shinning her

Asttarte Deva Shakti Bliss

blissful light into all who stop to head her sage counsel; can't wait for her next offering. Bliss & Ecstasy!" - Madame X, HP, Matriarch of the Dreaming, Producer of the Iron Garden, Prince of the Skylands Gateway Halo, author, teacher, muse & mystic.

Awaken to Living

Tantra for Your Whole Life

ASTTARTE DEVA

Asttarte Deva Shakti Bliss

Awaken to Living

Tantra for Your Whole Life

ASTTARTE DEVA

"Transformation" Cover painting by Jackie Hernandez

Asttarte Deva Publishing

First edition Copyright © 2018 by Asttarte Deva Shakti Bliss

All rights Reserved. No part of this publication may be reproduced without prior written permission from the author. This book is available at special quality discount for bulk purchases for sales premiums, fund-raising, and educational needs. For details, inquire with the publisher. Your ethical economic support of the authors intellectual rights is appreciated.

Awaken to Living; Tantra for Your Whole Life

"Transformation" Cover painting by Jackie Hernandez

http://artofjacqueline.wixsite.com/jacquelinehernandez

Painting on *Healing with the Chakras* Chapter done by Asttarte herself.

Excerpts from Love is a Stranger
Poetry of Mevlâna Jalâluddîn Rumi
Translated by **Kabir Helminski**
Versions by Coleman Barks of Unseen Rain

Tao De Ching by Stephen Mitchell

Printed by: CreateSpace & Asttarte Deva Publishing

ISBN # 13: 978-0692185858
ISBN # 10: 0692185852

Asttarte Deva is Also Published as a Featured Author in the following books:

How to Make Sacred Love to A Woman, An Intimate Exploration of Sacred Sexuality, by: Gabriel Morris

The Mystery of Woman; A Book for Men, by: Gabriel Morris

Recovering the Spirit; From Sexual Trauma; from the Traumatic to the Ecstatic, by: Kylie Devi

Asttarte Deva Shakti Bliss

Awaken to Living; Tantra for Your Whole Life

Contents

From My Beloved / 13
Introduction: An Orientation to Tantra, Including Warning / 17

Section 1:
The Beginning; Tantric Self and The Energy Body / 23
Chapter 1: The Patience of A Flower / 24
Chapter 2: The Courage to Heal / 25
Chapter 3: Purifying the Chakras / 27
Chapter 4: Eclectic Immersion of Bliss / 29
Chapter 5: Our Energy Bodies / 30
Chapter 6: The Yin and Yang of Energy / 32
Chapter 7: Awakening Bliss / 34
Chapter 8: The Importance of the Spirit Body Connection / 35
Chapter 9: When A Partner Lives Through Your Energy / 37
Chapter 10: The Breath to Stay IN the Body / 40
Chapter 11: The Energy Around the Body / 42
Chapter 12: Clearing the Energy Body / 44
Chapter 13: I Understand you Think Its Important to Cleanse My Energy, But I Still Just Don't Get It / 43
Chapter 14: The Spirit of Bliss / 46
Chapter 15: Increasing Your Vibrational Frequency 47
Chapter 16: What Color is Your Aura? / 49
Chapter 17: We Are Energy Magnets / 51
Chapter 18: Healing with The Chakras: Tantric & Kundalini Awakening / 53
Chapter 19: Purifying the Body / 57
Chapter 20: Awakening Passion with Art / 59
Chapter 21: Kundalini Orgasmic Meditation / 60

Section 2: Tantra Yoga / 63
Chapter 22: Unveiling the Eyes / 64
Chapter 23: Thoughts on Tantra / 66
Chapter 24: Tantra is Not The Easy Path / 68
Chapter 25: Tantra Yoga on the Mat / 70
Chapter 26: The Psychology of Tantra / 71
Chapter 27: Tantra As Self-Empowerment / 73

Chapter 28: Remembering Presence / 75
Chapter 29: Hug Therapy / 77
Chapter 30: What Is the Meaning of Tantra & Tantra Massage? / 78
Chapter 31: Tantra After the Holidays / 81
Chapter 32: Tantra & Patience / 83
Chapter 33: Tantra is Life: Tantra and the Misconception of the word Tantra / 86
Chapter 34: What Tantra is Not / 88
Chapter 35: The Sacred Arts: The Different Shades of Tantra / 90
Chapter 36: A Tantric Gift / 105
Chapter 37: Moon in Scorpio – Psychic Tantra / 107
Chapter 38: A Tantrikas Yoga Practice & being a Sexual Advocate Out in The World / 110

Section 3: Tantric Relationship / 113
Chapter 39: Re-directing Your Marriage; Finding Your Lost Commitment / 114
Chapter 40: Energetic Alignment in Relationships / 116
Chapter 41: Communication to Create the Intimacy You Really Want / 118
Chapter 42: Voicing Your Truth / 120
Chapter 43: Intimacy to Healing / 122
Chapter 44: Letting Your Heart Open / 123
Chapter 45: When You Want Your Husband and Someone Else Shows Up / 125
Chapter 46: Intimate Love with Your Partner / 126
Chapter 47: A Thriving Relationship / 128
Chapter 48: To Be Loved by A Man / 130
Chapter 49: Withholding Your Love / 134
Chapter 50: Your Partners Needs vs Yours / 135
Chapter 51: The Dominant Woman / 137
Chapter 52: Sexual Flirtations with Your Beloved / 139
Chapter 53: When You're In The Mood and Your Hunny Isn't / 140
Chapter 54: Heart Opening / 142
Chapter 55: Tantra and Intimacy / 144
Chapter 56: Pulling Passion Out of a Hat / 146
Chapter 57: Intimacy and Touch / 148
Chapter 58: Celebrating Spiritual Relationship / 149

Chapter 59: When To Go Past Dating / 151
Chapter 60: Letting Your Heart Open / 153

Section 4: Tantric Sex / 155
Chapter 61: How To Turn on Your Lover / 156
Chapter 62: Sexual Power / 158
Chapter 63: Unfolding Pleasure / 160
Chapter 64: Erectile Dysfunction – A Common Phenomenon / 161
Chapter 65: Why I Love Coconut Oil / 164
Chapter 66: The Cross Between Spirituality and Sexuality / 167
Chapter 67: Viagra vs Tantra Transformation / 168
Chapter 68: Desire After Being Single / 171
Chapter 69: Slow Sex is Best / 173
Chapter 70: Arousal as Energy Movement / 176
Chapter 71: Sex and Sadness / 178
Chapter 72: Sexual Repression to Expansion / 181
Chapter 73: Sexual Frustration and Open Marriage / 183
Chapter 74: Sex and Being Upset / 185
Chapter 75: Sexual Frustration and Anger / 188
Chapter 76: Sexual Energy and Stress / 190
Chapter 77: Grocery Shopping and Your Sexual Needs / 191
Chapter 78: When Your Hunny Just Doesn't Want to Have Sex / 193
Chapter 79: For the Guys – Your Prostate is Your Vitality / 194
Chapter 80: How Girls Can Keep Your Yoni Smelling Sweet; and not fishy (and guys who want to help)! / 196
Chapter 81: Venus and Sex / 199
Chapter 82: Choosing a Passionate Life / 204

Section 5: Professional Tantra / 207
Chapter 83: Boundaries in Intimacy / 208
Chapter 84: The Energy of Love / 210
Chapter 85: The Differences Between Tantra Yoga, Sexual Healing and Intimacy Therapy / 212
Chapter 86: The Many Types of Tantra Healing / 215
Chapter 87: Description of a Dakini / 226
Chapter 88: The Gentler Side of Tantra / 227
Chapter 89: Sacred Foot Massage / 229
Chapter 90: How All Sessions Go / 231

Chapter 91: Knowing Your Intention / 233

Section 6: Tantric Prayer / 235
Chapter 92: To Cleanse and Purify Energy / 236
Chapter 93: Buddhism and Hinduism Tantra Masters / 238

Section 7: Tantric Men / 245
Chapter 94: Gratitude for the Guys / 246
Chapter 95: Angry Cock / 248

Section 8: Tantric Asttarte / 251
Chapter 96: A True Tantrikas Journey / 252
Chapter 97: Remembering Presence / 256
Chapter 98: Psychic Sexual Healer / 258
Chapter 99: Practice Based on Love / 261
Chapter 100: A Little About Me and Some Thoughts / 263

Section 9: Poetry / 267
Radiating Everywhere, a poem / 269
Just Allow / 271
Pleasure with All Your Clothes On / 273
Relationship Manifestation / 275
Being Present / 277
The Love of a Stranger, a poem, by Asttarte Deva / 279
Vulnerability into Pleasure / 281
Detachment, Surrender, Acceptance / 283
Spiritual Poetry on Love / 285
Servant of Peace – Prayer of St Francis / 287

Section 10: Testimonials / 289
Excerpt: Remembering Rama / 300
Section 11: About the Author / 303

From my Beloved

In 2016 after a 32-year marriage to my friend and mother to my three beautiful children, I discovered that I was unhappy, repressed, depressed, angry that my life was coming to an end and I wanted to die of loneliness. Until one cold November night when I decided to google Tantra Philadelphia, I discovered what might be the answer to my unhappiness. Asttarte Deva popped up and I began to read most of her amazing blogs that actually make up this compilation of writing that you will read in this book. Well, after an eight-hour night of fascination, and intrigued reading, every blog and video she has produced, I knew that we had to meet. The next morning when I actually called Asttarte, as nervous as a young boy, dreaming to have a fulfilling and happy life, Asttarte answered the phone. Wow, it only took a few minute conversation before I jumped into my car and raced over to have a short meeting, cup of tea of course, and to see as though Asttarte could teach me to live a new life of lessons and allow me to reverse a life of unhappiness. When we first met, and I walked into her house, it was only after a few short minutes that I realized I found home.

I was mesmerized just listening and holding every word out of her mouth – as I stood up and shook her hand good bye – I made an immediate decision to sign up for a six-month Coaching commitment.

Ok, I will now tell the readers of her book of blogs that this woman is the most magical, spiritual and experienced Intuitive Healer on the planet.

We spent six months twice a week on the most intense sessions imaginable. Every session flew by as though time was against me. I would leave each session blown away with this new life that I was about to blossom.

The heart, the breath, chakra work, every modality that Asttarte used in our sessions brought me closer to my heart that I didn't know up until now even existed. Never in my life did I believe that I would find a practitioner who could help me move through that stagnant energy, repression, depression, and dark relationships all my life.

To a life of opening my heart, forgiving the past, healing myself, transforming me spiritually, emotionally and sexually. Once the six months were over something happened. I knew I could not be married anymore. The miracle happened. Asttarte and I on our last session of her amazing Spiritual Coaching - we stood there ready to say our good byes and to my amazement she took a leaping jump and landed in my arms. To only find out one week later that Asttarte discovered against all of her boundaries dating a client and said I must fire you and if you decide to end your unhappy marriage, I would like to spend a lifetime with a real man like yourself.

We have spent almost 2 years together, over 10 Shamanic Journeys, countless hours of eye gazing, cuddling, Chakra work, Ascension Meditation, Thai Yoga Massage, Tantra Training, Transformation work, Breathwork, making many videos and audios together, and don't let me forget, Jin Shin Do Bodymind Acupressure.

I sit here now, writing a Forward for my lifetime beloved, thanking our angels for connecting us at a time our planets perfectly aligned.

I want to mention that since 1983, when I received my MSW from Temple University, I have worked with countless number of men and women through my Horticulture Therapy Practice. I've had 30 Years as a Sponsor in 12 Step Work, Mankind, ACOA, my own therapist the great Bill Lundgren, and my experience and Training in Breema Therapy. I've had many years of Yoga and Meditation, Spiritual Prayer and Intention, if you read Asttarte's book, you will see that she lives and breathes every moment of her life working to help all of humanity to learn to love themselves and live a happy and Blissful life.

~ Paul Cook, MSW, Horticulturist and Plant Therapist

Asttarte Deva Shakti Bliss

Introduction: An Orientation to Tantra

Awaken to Living; Tantra for Your Whole Life is an awakening into your whole self. It's a compilation of writings I wrote of my journey as a Healer and my practice of giving to others and how it can expand yourself into spiritual awakening, and profound joy and bliss. In the beginning of my journey as a Tantric Healer, I had less boundaries and less awareness of how other people's energies impacted my own as I do now. As I have progressed into my own path and have healed deeper aspects of my soul and am now with the man of my dreams, those boundaries have changed. This is the first book of a series of many on the realms of energy healing, emotional healing, empowering relationships, spirituality, tantra for couples, healing for women, energy work and more.

In this book, you will read many articles written from the eyes of a Dakini; a Shamanic Sacred Sexual Healer, Intuitive, and Tantrica. Many writings are from 2007, 2008, 2009, and 2010. Some are more recent. This work has helped me heal myself, and it too will help you heal you. You will read some poetry, stories of love, heart opening, tools for expanding your capacity to feel, and coaching practices in the realms of sexual energy, sexual healing, awakening the sexual self, loving another in an intimate sexual way, and the types of practices that may help you in expanding yourself to open your chakras, and energy centers for expanded bliss and pleasure.

The Way to Use This Book:

This book is broken up in Eleven sections. The first section is on the topic of The Tantric Self and the Energy Body. This has to do with the individual person and how they exist in the world as an energetic human being. It has to do with their true individual self as the natural energetic being of who they are, including the importance of being with oneself, healing oneself, and how each person has an energy body and how that energy body exists in the world around them. It has to do with how their energetic self can be cleansed and purified, how this energetic self can get stagnant and stuck, the awakening of a human being through energy practices, and the basic foundations of what energy is all about. It has to do with how one's energy body can be affected by the world around them, and different practices that may support one to cleanse their energy self to be more at ease and comfortable living in their own body being in a world of chaos and stress.

The second section of the book is on the topic of Tantra Yoga, what Tantra Yoga is, how one can use Tantra Yoga to connect deeper to their pure self, and to another. It explains how Tantra is a lifestyle and the psychology of tantra at its core of an emotional healing process. It addresses what Tantra Massage is, what Tantra is and what it is not and how to use it to empower oneself. **I WARN YOU** on an article in this section called the Sacred Arts; The Different Shades of Tantra. This is written as an experienced Energy Worker working in the realms of sexual energy. For those with Religious Affiliation, this section perhaps may question your beliefs, or make you feel judgment. I ask you to please open your mind and heart, and read with the possibility that anything is possible, and some of this information may not be found anywhere out there. However, you may also find this article entertaining and educational on the aspects of personal growth.

The third section of the book is on Tantric Relationships and can be used as a guide to help your intimate and significant relationship in your life. The topics discussed won't be relevant for everyone, but they will be relevant to many. Some topics here are to cleanse your energy within a relationship, creating intimacy in a relationship, using your voice and communication to create closeness, sexual frustration in a long-term commitment, opening your heart, creating passion and strengthening Intimacy. I also added an article that's been published in other books I was featured in, called *To Be Loved By A Man*, so it deserved to be here as well.

The fourth section of this book is focused on Tantric Sex, how to harness tantric sex, how to increase one's sexual energy and sexual power, and major issues that show up in a relationship that impact their sex life. Also included are the connections between sex being a spiritual practice and a sexual practice, how you can use Tantra to open your energy centers and connect to how emotions show up in sexual connection.

Section Five is on working as a Professional Tantric Practitioner, the boundaries, always standing from a place of love and what working with a practitioner looks like, how sessions go, different types of sessions and what the healing work is all about.

Section Six is a short section of Tantra, Mantra and Prayers, Section 7 is on Tantric Men and Section 8 is on Asttarte as a Tantrica.

Section 9 is a few poems that have been published online and in other manuscripts, and 8 have been written by Asttarte, and also includes a poem by Rumi, a piece from the Tao and The Prayer of St Francis.

Section 10 includes many testimonials of old clients who worked with Asttarte and got tremendous results, and lastly Section 11 is a section on About the Author, and the last section includes an article eulogy on a friend who passed Dec 10, 2011.

Asttarte Deva Shakti Bliss

Read this section first before you move on to reading the rest of the book.

You want to be aware that when you begin to read a book on Tantra, and one that includes more knowledge, background, history, and detailed experiences, it is very important that you are aware of the potential triggers that may show up for you. Not everyone can handle the depth of intensity of tantra and without full knowledge of what you are getting yourself into, you may be exposing yourself to things you are not quite ready for.

Some knowledge of tantra is more elaborate and detailed than others, especially from teachers that have had more intensive experience, training and exposure to the full range of all levels and degrees of tantra, and in this case, many levels of spiritual development and healing as well. Some people who choose to learn tantra, may have a background of sexual trauma, abuse, sexual or not, or may have emotional, verbal and psychic abuse from generations of family repressing their full expression as a sexual, and vibrant human being. Some family and religious backgrounds shun the notion of sexual expression, feel it wrong, and reprimand, demean, ridicule, and condemn those who try to be fully free in their bodies, and enjoy the expression as a human being. If you have any background from your family, your religious upbringing, your extended family, or your adolescence and childhood that shunned you, learning tantra and the ability to transform your spiritual and sexual self may be at first a shock and difficult to understand the true depth of meaning and understanding in the deepest parts of your soul.

If you want to become fully enlightened in all levels of your being, learning tantra, yoga and spiritual awakening is the most beautiful and fulfilling path you could journey on. However, one must first begin to learn the basic tenets and notions of the emotional psyche, as well as the spiritual energy of a human being, before embarking on the deeper meanings of tantra. If those of you who are reading this book now have not had basic knowledge or deeper knowledge of spirituality, extensive psychological training, spiritual development, psychotherapy, a long practice of yoga, the breath, the chakras, and your frequency and energy system, trying to understand tantra and the advanced path of yoga and tantric teachings will not be easily comprehended.

I wish for you to study everything you can possibly grab your hands on to fully advance yourself as a spiritual human being, and for those of you who have had a background of repression or trauma, I wish for you to get the healing, support, and training necessary to build your foundation of your spiritual self, and along the way, learn the concepts of the advanced arts of tantra in this book and find love along the way.

Love,

Asttarte Deva

Section 1
The Beginning; Tantric Self and The Energy Body

1
The Patience of a Flower

When a flower is in its beginning stages, it first must take root before it can grow. It first takes the idea; the intention to plant it, then it takes time to develop under the soil and realize the potential it has before it even begins to develop, it takes on a form of its own; an identity and begins to birth an energy within it. Then it slowly has life and starts to sprout from underground moving its way to the surface, and over time the flower builds a vine, that of which it can stand tall upon, and then it develops its bud, which slowly blooms into a petal and lays out its wings in utter beauty!

When planting a bulb, it takes patience before it turns into a flower. When transforming yourself from your history, trauma and turmoil, it takes the patience of a lion. When transforming yourself in your intimate relationship, it takes the patience of a bull. May we all become lions and bulls with ourselves, each other and our lives!

2 The Courage To Heal

It takes a lot of courage to look at oneself; to be vulnerable, willing to express your fears, sadness, pain or struggles. Most people would rather keep their fears to themselves, and put on the image of looking good, doing great, and feeling fine, when inside the truth is they are not fine and their desire to look good and be doing great to others is only what's covering up how they are really feeling.

When issues come up in the moment, the most powerful way to get past them is to go through them, not over them, under them or pulling away from them. The best way to overcome something is to dive straight through it.

When anger arises, be with it. Experience your full self as the anger and live into the anger, nurture the anger, caress the anger and allow it to come out of you. Many people who have a lot of anger inside them try to control it and then all of a sudden it bursts out like a canon ball and explodes all over the place. Some people drink or exercise to get rid of the emotion, but it is still there underneath and always will be until it is dealt with, and faced head on.

The best way to be with the anger, is to let it out - - punching pillows, screaming into pillows, doing breathwork that lets the rage/anger/whatever emotion it is **come out**. Looking at yourself in the mirror and screaming to get it out, punching with fists to express your emotion and stand your ground that this is how you feel, and you know it is true for you, no matter what anyone else thinks, and you honor that feeling, be with it, express it, without putting it on anyone else. Then you can be free of it, and it won't affect any of your relationships.

When sadness arises, the best way to heal the sadness is to let the sadness know it is just as important as any other emotion. It has a purpose and reason for being there and it will teach you and help you grow. When healing sadness, love the sadness, nurture it, spend time with it, journaling, doing breathwork, talking about it, sitting in front of the mirror and practicing eye gazing with yourself and breathing into your heart, going for walks in nature, getting a massage/ energy healing/ acupressure or acupuncture session, taking flower essences, and breathing into the sadness, being with it and loving it. It will eventually move through you and you will come back to your integrated full self. And, in the process be able to help others who are going through similar pains.

Sometimes when healing yourself, it is important to take time to be alone. And, sometimes it is also important to have people you can talk to.

Healing in healthy ways, no matter what the issue or feeling you are dealing with, is the most effective and productive way to grow!

Other excellent techniques are some that were mentioned in the article prior to this. Flower Essence Therapy and EFT is highly recommended.

3 Purifying the Chakras

Welcome to the gift of your spirit, the zest for life, a nurturing energy that purifies the heart, opens your throat, your speaking and creativity, your intuition, your wisdom, your passion for love, and a center to ground you to your truth once again. When one's chakras are clouded, mucky, and stuck, so too is one's life, their heart and their spirit and the energy that brings one's journey to feel nurtured, loved, fulfilling and supportive of their true calling; their passion and drive and the very source of what makes life worth living.

I love how spirit reminds me of the importance to be pure, and when I am not, life shows up as the same. As I purify myself, and my energy is thriving, so too is all life around me. Each chakra has a significant importance to a very specific area of your life, your energy, your bodies flow, the emotional nature you are made up of, and the very core thing that drives you to be as natural and authentic as you!

There are many books on the chakras, and many teachers who bring wisdom of insight on the chakras. However, I like to remind those with interest, the importance and relevance the chakras have on every single aspect of our lives, and how all parts of our lives are impacted by the level of clarity our chakras exist in. You may find knowledge on the chakras through yoga, or chi gung, or reiki, Taoism, Chinese medicine, Ayurveda, massage, different religions, books on meditation, health, psychology, and many others. However, not one will be more right than the other. They all have wisdom and they all have truth.

"To be pure is to be you, and to be you is the greatest gift life has to offer!"
When we are clouded, we are letting life control us. When we take the time to become clear, and pure, we bring a freshness to life that offers a new set of eyes each and every time we cleanse ourselves to our wholeness again! Choose to be clear, and you

choose to be you! I will choose me over and over again! I hope you too, choose your true self every time!

The root chakra, anchors you to the earth, helps one feel secure, connected to their bodies and the world around them.

The second or sacral chakra is one's center of creativity, their relationship portal and the openness or closeness one has to be intimate with others.

The third or solar plexus, is one's control and power center, and the area one allows to be controlled by others or to choose to take control of one's life in their own hands.

The heart or 4th chakra, the area of giving and receiving love, the most basic human need, and yet often the one many block or resist out of fear, sadness or worry.

The 5th or throat chakra, the area of ones speaking their voice, their truth, to be heard what is deep inside of them, and the place their creativity leaves the body.

The 6th or third eye center, where one can see the future, their intuition, inner wisdom, insight, ability to trust in the unknown, and receive spiritual guidance and messages.

The crown or 7th chakra, where one is connected to spirit, God, the infinite and the essence to all that is; where one feels the openness to their innocence and the sacredness to the divine.

I am grateful for another opportunity to be cleared, and a vehicle to open the door to wisdom, and a place for my creativity to be opened and anchored in the world! I hope you all have a chance to create clarity for yourselves and the support to allow the purity to unravel. If not, let us set the tone for another opportunity to grow!

4 Eclectic Immersion of Bliss

To live fully unto yourself is its natural state of the child you were born into. Once you learn the pleasures of life, you can never go back to the state you were before. And, as such, when children get bombarded by the control of our society, a level of brainwashing takes effect.

We grow up feeling as if we are truly living our passion, or truly living what we love, but we later learn we are suppressed, frustrated and angry. There are layers and layers of patterns that get built, and as our perceptions of the world change, so do our beliefs; about who we are, why we are here, and what really matters to us. We transition and stop being the free spirits we once were. We grow to have fears, limitations, boundaries, and restrictions; just as the rules we grew up with around us and in our society.

This work is about removing those layers, unraveling so to speak and peeling back the parts of your self that have covered you up so that you can live into the true essence that you are; your divinity, your innocence, your love and your bliss!

When you can open up, and surrender your body to your spirit, your heart to your soul, and your mind to your heart, you can be anything, and truly live a bliss filled life!

5 Our Energy Bodies

How subtle our energy bodies are when we look outside of ourselves at another human being without saying a word, and suddenly that someone looks our way and notices how amazing they feel just by gazing upon us. No words were spoken - the only thing that based their decision to reach out to us was how they felt. It was their intuition that guided them to choose to be open to us, or to walk away. That intuition was their energy body communicating to your energy body in such a way that it felt safe, or familiar, or exciting. Nothing else made them know that they would like you or be comfortable with you. All they know is what they felt.

Everyone's energy body is speaking a different language. We are all at different vibrations radiating different levels of frequency and energy that goes out into the universe and the universe, or others, respond accordingly. All people on the planet are attracted to others based on their energy body. The energy body speaks many languages. We are all carrying certain energies that match our beliefs, our history, our traumas, our desires and our fears. Most people on the planet are intuitive; some more so than others. However, the more open our energy bodies are to positive and healthy vibrations, the more we will attract positive and healthy individuals in our lives. Often as we expand and heal, others close to us will as well. And those who do not, that we cherish and love, who stay stagnant, sometimes will be left behind as our energies will then travel on different passages since the attraction and compatibility changes.

To achieve a state of bliss, you must be ready - emotionally, mentally, physically and spiritually. When you can learn to expand your spiritual body, cleansing it, purifying it, then your physical body will be ready to move on to gaining access to the bliss that awaits you underneath the (what I like to call)

energetic clutter. All levels of your being are important, and before you can awaken your kundalini power; to your tantric and blissful essence, your spiritual body **must** be ready to achieve it.

6 The Yin & Yang of Energy

Balancing energies of our own energy body vehicle; our inner selves with our outer selves is what will ultimately allow others to achieve the state of ecstatic bliss one often reads about.

Our inner self is our mind, our thoughts and our emotions, as well as the energy within our bodies. This includes the energy in our muscle tissues, our fibers, our meridian channels, our spinal column, our organs and most importantly the chakras up and down our bodies. The Tantra Kundalini Awakening Breathwork practice or practices can allow some of this energy to be opened, but it is also important to do personal psychotherapy on oneself, as well as chakra meditations, energy healing and any modalities to release the energy within the body.

As the energy within is opened, purified and cleansed the wave of bliss can flow more easily up and down your energy channel, as well as in and out of your pores, your breath and your chakras.

Our outer selves; the energy around the body, the auric field, the energy body or whatever you wish to call it also needs to be purified. As the energy outside your physical body is cleansed it allows you to feel more of your sensations on your physical body. The chakras reside within the body and outside the body, so it is important to clear the entire chakra; not just inside, but also outside, and intend, visualize and imagine it pure. As you see areas of darkness, ask for it to be released, and visualize the beautiful color of that chakra radiating its beauty.

As your entire energy field around your body is cleared, there becomes a synchronistic flow of energy that waves from within your body to the outside, and from the top of your body to the bottom. In and out, up and down, and flows all around. As this energy is clear, all possibilities and energy flowing can be achieved, and this then is the state we all wish to feel, experience and aliven. It allows a deep feeling of ecstasy and bliss that most only read about, and few have the privilege of achieving.

This is what I teach. This is what I offer. I offer you balance; from within to without and the flow of energy you carry to be cleared, purified and then awakened to the state of pure utter energetic ecstasy! This is my gift to you!

7 Awakening Bliss

"In order to access your full potential of bliss,
you have to clear the muck that's in the way!"

We are all Spiritual beings living in a physical body. Our spiritual body is mostly unknown to people on the planet; except those who are conscious and on the path. It is my pleasure and joy to work with those who are on the path, and to those who are not, to learn the power and value in getting started.

I offer you many techniques and practices that took me many years to learn and practice, and many more to master. It is the utmost importance to allow the spirit to be of a significant factor in your journey of reflection, your recovery to healing, your awakening to the divine, and your passionate desire to connect to others.

Bliss is not something that can be achieved through simple pleasures of the ego, the mind or the body. Bliss is achieved through connecting to something much bigger than we all are - the metaphysical, transcendental, ethereal and energetic part of ourselves that lies not only inside of us, but all around us. Achieving bliss is a state of mind through conscious efforts in connecting to our spiritual selves.

   Bliss can be achieved through the body, but there are always energetic blocks that keep us from fully expanding and opening into a higher vibration that our divine being is craving for us to embrace. When we can merge the physical body with the spiritual body, we can then achieve a full body state of ecstatic bliss.

8 The Importance of The Spirit Body Connection

The Spiritual Energetic Body is just as important as our passionate desires of the physical body. Our energy being carries as much energy in it as does our passions and needs for life. And in fact, they are one in the same. Our spiritual centers carry messages and memories in them, that if not cleansed, nurtured or healed, affect us for the rest of our lives. Our energy or spiritual body carries with us the remainder of what physically happened to us in the past, and how our emotional body and mental body processed the information. What we get left with days, weeks, and even years after an event happened is the result of the stress that remains with us from before, and as a result, it stays in our vibrational system that can either make us sick, create unhealthy patterns in our life, or can even cause diseases, or cancers.

Most people just accept life as it happens, and choose to move on ignoring the event that happened to us. Then all of a sudden, you are caught in a trap of a cycle that eludes you and takes control over your life. An example is: you and your wife argue all the time. You come to disagreements in almost every conversation. You haven't gotten to the bottom of why these arguments happen and both people feel unloved, unappreciated, unaccepted and invalidated as a person. Then your hormones increase, and you want to make love, but your wife is uninterested because of all the arguments you had, or you are no longer turned on because you are tired of fighting. Then nothing gets accomplished and neither persons needs are met. The relationship becomes stagnant and distant. Another example is: you are working at a job where you give up your life to take care of others. You end up, in a sense, giving up yourself and ultimately giving up your identity. You start out by being exhausted all the time. You have no time for a social life because all you want to do is rest when you are alone. Your children never see you. Your husband or wife starts getting used to you never being around, and you lose the connection you worked so hard to achieve. Eventually you start getting other symptoms that could lead to a heart attack, a stroke, a nervous breakdown, migraines, or worse a form of cancer.

There are many examples I could use; however, the point is that we all carry energy from our past, be it an hour before, a week before, or a month before. And the most powerful way of creating a sacred connection with the one you love, or your tantra practitioner, is to either cleanse your energy before coming to the session, or doing a form of cleansing ritual while you are in session before getting started in the Tantra or Sexual Healing work. The connection is much more powerful when both people are clear of anything in the past, and even more so when they are both in a high vibration of spiritual love. When there is a repeated pattern of separation in a relationship, it is best to seek therapy, as well as do the energy clearing before connecting to making love, but the connection is stronger the more you can be rid of what happened from the past. Being in the moment truly means being free of anything that's keeping you, your mind or your body out of the present moment. The best ways to cleanse one's energy is through meditation, energy clearing practices, any other forms of energy healing, yoga, acupuncture, and many others. If you are interested in a more Spiritual & Psycho-therapeutic form of healing not mentioned, please contact me and we will discuss options. These sessions are not tantric and have no intention other than your health, wellness, energy balancing and psychological growth.

9 When A Partner Lives Through Your Energy

People come together for many reasons, and sometimes we never know what those reasons are. Often times when we first meet someone we are vibrating at a certain frequency that matches with the person we are drawn to and there is an alignment that fills a need, and when we're lucky feels loving and fulfilling.

When we've worked through the patterns in our self that caused us to be attracted to someone else, we often grow away from the other person. Or we may no longer need them in the way we did before. Sometimes the roles get reversed, and the person you were originally pursuing, then starts pursuing you instead as they feel your need for them is missing. Your need for them is what had originally kept them attached to you. They needed you, in a sense, to need them. However, when you change and stop needing them, the part of them that craved your needing them is no longer filled and becomes empty.

When you pull away, instead of pushing toward, they may become angry, or confused, or depressed.

In the past, you may have surrendered to their need, and instead of pulling away further, you may have felt bad and wanted to sooth their pain, so you compromised your own need to detach. However, when you give in to their power, their need to pull you in, you also give up your control, your self worth, your self-esteem and your confidence. Immediately when you recognize this pattern and detach from them, you'll feel better; vibrant, alive, refreshed and energized.

This is related to the third chakra, and when you allow another to pull on your energy, in a sense, and suck you in while they are depleting you, you yourself become depressed, weak, angry, and lack confidence, self worth AND self esteem. The third chakra gets completely out of control. As soon you cut your connection to them energetically, after recognizing this is happening, you will feel yourself again, and then THEY may become the person who in truth has low self-esteem, low self-worth, lack of confidence, and a lot of anger. However, all you did was detach from them. It is not you who truly had these issues. It was truly them, and your allowing them to pull on you and overpower your energy will keep you in the cycle of feeling these things in yourself instead.

If the other person, or your ex-partner is not doing their inner work and continues to try to live through your chakras, you will continue to feel energetically repressed and overpowered again and again. One MUST protect them-selves in order for this dynamic to stop happening, AND be aware when it is happening.

This may also be in the same bracket as Abusive Relationships, Narcissism, and Self Sabotage. Are you used to being abused? Are you used to allowing others to control you? Have you been abused as a child and are still living out this pattern as an adult with the partners you choose? The only way to clear this is to recognize it is happening, and to constantly cleanse myself, to stand your ground, protect yourself, and OFTEN, walk away.
Sometimes the only people who can recognize that this pattern is happening, are psychics, intuitive's and healers, but when you yourself are also a Healer, or work with energy; you may forget that you too are living in this same dynamic.

What must be done is to cleanse and cut the cords, immediately upon recognition. Wearing protective stones, taking protection essences, protective bracelets, amulets for protection, doing cleansing rituals and baths, meditating, working with another healer, constantly cutting the cords in the chakras that are attached and other practices that are helpful is a daily, if not weekly spiritual practice. Prayer is the best medicine, and with a little help, and persistence, the patterns can end, and the other person will stop trying to feed through your energy.

We only wish that these people heal their inner selves and discover for themselves what is missing in them that they must feed off of your own energy, however, when they don't listen, and refuse to do their work, the only solution, is to detach. And when necessary to see them, detaching, again, and again, and again. And truly truly live!

10 The Breath to Stay IN the Body

The breath is a very powerful tool. Most people don't know how powerful it is until they embark on a Yoga path, start doing Breathwork, receive energy healing sessions, or begin the Advanced practices of Tantra.

Often when someone is receiving a massage, it is not the massage that is completely relaxing them, it is the massage that creates a stimulation in the body to remind the person to come into the body and to take deeper breaths. Ultimately, from taking these deeper breaths, this then is what causes the person to be able to have a fully relaxing and blissful experience during the massage. However, some people who receive massage, may have the most skilled and advanced practitioner working on them, but when they do not breathe properly, are holding their breath, or are not guided in breathing deeply when they may need to, their experience can be rather dull, and they may think it's the practitioner who was not very good, when in fact it was in their own creation of not using their breath to its maximum potential.

When I work in Session with my private clients, I often remind my client to breath deeply. The breath can be a means of escaping the body. Many times, when someone is holding their breath, forgets to breath, or falls fast into a deep relaxation when we are doing powerful breathing exercises to raise the Kundalini, or to allow for a deeper sensation of pleasure, this means that there is something blocking the person from going deeper into the practice. When someone slips away from the breath, it is often a slipping away and out of the body as well. This happens when there is a deep emotion, or issue that is ready to come to the surface and wants to be released, but the individual does not know how to deal with it, and instead reacts by suppressing it further and pushing it down, by not breathing or breathing shallow.

By escaping their own body, they are also escaping the fear or pain of what wants to come up to be released, energetically moved or cleared for them. This fear or pain often is unknown of. It doesn't necessarily need to be something you even know what it is, but when a numbness in the body, or detachment from the body by slipping into shallow breathing happens, this is the exact time you need to be conscious of your breath and begin to breath with more awareness and attention to actively breathe deeper.

Why is being in the body something you want to work towards? Because you will then get to release the block in your vibration, your mind, your emotions and your entire energetic system, and this then will allow you to move into deeper presence in your own body, experiencing pleasure, sensations that you could not even feel before, and an opening in your heart and the ability to love others and receive others more deeply. Doesn't everyone want to feel more of what they are capable of? Why not let go of what is keeping you from experiencing bliss and allow the breath to be your tool to access it!!!

11 The Energy Around The Body

In some of my Tantra Yoga classes and training, we learned about doing energy scans and clearing energy with another in your presence, sitting across from each other, standing across from one another or in other dynamics. As an Energy Healer for over 21 years, I take this energy clearing a step beyond just the simple energy scans that I learned in Tantra classes.

There is a direct connection to embracing in love as there is in one's energy field being pure, cleansed and sacred. When one has an energy field of pure essence, the divine connection of union can be then manifest into a warm deep embrace of love. It is not only I who needs to have pure and clear energy, but it is also you. As your energy is purified, and mine is clear, the deep utter embrace of intimate healing of love happens. I only open my physical body temple to the level of openness you have in yours.

Cleansing one's energy field can either be an easy task, or may be necessary to spend a larger amount of time nurturing. If you are generally living a stress-free life, and are mostly happy, then cleansing your energy field is an easy job. However, if you are extremely stressed, carrying weight on your shoulders from your marriage, your partnership, other relationships or work, then it may take more work to develop the sacred union of intimacy through tantric touch, intimacy healing and sexual healing that you may perhaps be pursuing. I may do a brief energy scan on your body as you enter into my Healing Temple, however, if you are dealing with larger psychological issues then we may need to go deeper, and spend more time on the layers of clouds that are living around your body.

An energy field is like a dirty diamond that once washed can shine to its purist beauty. And, as humans living in physical form, we are like sponges that take on layers of stress in our daily lives, and until that stress is removed it will linger around your body waiting to be purified and released.

12 Clearing The Energy Body

There are many tools and paths to clearing the energy body, but what's most important is that you use the tools available. Most don't know the value of clearing the energy body, let alone, how one goes about doing it. Clearing the Energy Body, is a celebration and a renewal to the real self that is sitting and waiting for you to awaken.

Many practices I mention are excellent ways of clearing the energy body; such as chakra clearing and balancing, IET, all types of Reiki, and energy healing, meditation, and breathwork. Other tools are emotional release work, massage therapy, and yoga.

When one clears the energy body, they can connect to the wave of bliss waiting inside themselves and as the outside awakens to the inside, the inside then merges back out again with the outside. The energy of the entire person then flows in a spiral from the internal to the external; the physical body, to the energetic body, the feeling of touch to the skin, to the senses of one's energy and auric field all around them. The whole person then experiences a wave of bliss and love and a connection to all that is, is achieved.

13 I Understand You Think It's Important to cleanse my energy, but I still just don't get it

The Spiritual Body carries memories in it, and almost anyone who has any bit of intuition can feel how you are feeling. If you come in with a load of baggage from a day's amount of stress or a year's amount of stress, it can be felt, and the best and most amazing feeling of connection to have with another is when that weight of stress is minimized or eliminated completely.

When you go on vacation and get away from your problems you can feel the opening and peacefulness all around you. When you surround yourself around others who take your mind off of your stresses, you can forget the problem, but the problem is still there waiting for you to return to. One tiny little memory can take you back to the exact thing that you are totally frustrated or unhappy with, and the weight of stress sits right back on your shoulders again.

It is not easy to cleanse one's spiritual body, especially in a private 2 hour session, however, getting started is most important. Even giving it one hour to cleanse yourself, and one hour to work on the area of your desire is better than not doing it at all. Honestly, I don't want to work with others where their priority is not to evolve their spiritual bodies or awaken their consciousness on a higher level. However, if they are willing to have an open mind and learn, I am open to working with them.

14 The Spirit of Bliss

"In order to access your full potential of bliss,
you have to clear the muck that's in the way!

We are all Spiritual beings living in a physical body. Our spiritual body is mostly unknown to people on the planet; except those who are conscious and on the path. It is my pleasure and joy to work with those who are on the path, and to those who are not, to learn the power and value in getting started.

I offer you many techniques and practices on this website that took me many years to learn and practice, and many more to master. It is the utmost importance to allow the spirit to be of a significant factor in your journey of reflection, your recovery to healing, your awakening to the divine, and your passionate desire to connect to others.

Bliss is not something that can be achieved through simple pleasures of the ego, the mind or the body. Bliss is achieved through connecting to something much bigger than we all are - the metaphysical, transcendental, ethereal and energetic part of ourselves that lies not only inside of us, but all around us. Achieving bliss is a state of mind through conscious efforts in connecting to our spiritual selves.

Bliss can be achieved through the body, but there are always energetic blocks that keep us from fully expanding and opening into a higher vibration that our divine being is craving for us to embrace. When we can merge the physical body with the spiritual body, we can then achieve a full body state of ecstatic bliss.

15 Increasing Your Vibrational Frequency

Perhaps you are unfamiliar with this terminology, however, as a Reiki Master Teacher, Yoga Teacher, IET Advanced Healer, Frequency Balancing Practitioner, Axiotonal Alignment Practitioner and igili Angel Healer, there is no way I can avoid telling you the power of increasing your vibration, or offering to teach it. Even more, I cannot possibly ignore that I have this wealth of knowledge to offer you, and sit back sharing nothing and keeping it hidden.

That would be selfish of me. This information is like a goldmine of abundance of bliss and peacefulness that can be harnessed and created from within your own body vehicle, and I will do everything I can to share this information with my clients, offer you these practices to achieve these states of bliss and peacefulness and continue to show you my love by accepting where you are in your journey. Please don't pass up the opportunity to receive a Healing Session from me. I know you all love Tantra and want to experience the benefits of increased pleasure, but without the increase of your vibration, you'll never know what you are missing.

Increasing your vibrational frequency is increasing your access to the divine and your ability to be truly present in the moment. It is removing the weight around your body and gaining access to the light being that you were born into on this planet. It is a way to connect to your soul and your angelic nature. It is when you feel at one with all things and all of life. It is your natural self, free of all limitations, purified of your ego, your needs and desires, and your innocent gentleness returning to you. It is when your physical body and your spiritual body intertwine, and you feel weightless to life and there is no separation between your body and the space all around you. It is truly a living experience of bliss in your body now!

You'll have to come with a no expectation mind-set in your journey, and expect nothing but an increase in your energy vibration, your overall health and well-being and deeper peace within yourself.

The end result is you'll start opening your energy channels and bring in a higher vibration of love.

16 What Color is Your Aura?

Do you know what color your aura is? Do you know what color your energy is vibrating? Do you know what frequency the energy your aura is vibrating?

Have you ever looked at an animal at peace, resting at home, and noticed the color he or she was putting off? Have you ever tried looking closely at your lover when they were upset, and noticed the color they emitted from their body?

When someone is at peace, they are going to put off a certain frequency and a certain color or colors that reflect the peace they are feeling. The same goes for when someone is upset; they are going to reflect in their energetic space, the colors that they are feeling.

For instance, when someone is feeling peaceful, quiet and gentle, you may notice their colors as green, blue or white. And, when they are upset, they may have more colors such as red, orange, even gray or black, or a foggy yellow or dark blue. The dominant color when someone is upset is red or orange, and the dominant color when someone is at peace is blue, green or white. Before even speaking to someone, you may be able to sense or pick up how they are feeling before beginning a conversation. Sometimes this is helpful when you know they may be feeling sensitive, or you are going to have a serious conversation. You may, in a sense, know how they are going to respond before speaking, or perhaps know how to speak in a way that may be supportive to the person's reaction.

How do you change the color of your aura?

Once you are aware of the dominant colors you are putting off in the world, and you are aware of the meaning behind the colors, you can then choose, if you desire, to put off a different frequency and a different emotion into the world. The best way to change into a different frequency, is to choose "how is it I want to be feeling today?" And, make a statement to yourself, "I am choosing today to be happy, vibrant and to feel alive!" How might those colors reflect in the world? It might be a bright beautiful orange, a vibrant yellow, a soft or loud pink, and perhaps blue or green. We don't get to choose the colors we put off, but we do get to choose how we want to feel, and then choose practices to support us to feel more in alignment with that choice. It takes practice to shift how we are feeling, but with practice, it can become easy.

People really do need people to support each other in this world, and sometimes, when you are stuck in a dark cloud, or dark aura, asking for guidance is the best solution.
Other positive statements might be something like this:
"I am grounded, secure and powerful in the world. I love who I am, and people love me!"

"I am a passionate being, I am creative, and my creativity is a magnet for success, joy and love!"

"I love who I am, and I love what I do! People love who I am and love being with me!"

"I am a beautiful, kind human being, and that is enough! I can be me and that is awesome!"

If you know how you are feeling, you have more of an access for choosing to vibrate at a different frequency and a different color. If you would like to read more on the aura, colors and frequency, let me know. I'll write more pieces to support you and your understanding, growth and creativity!

17
We Are Energy Magnets

What kind of energy have you taken on lately? What experiences have you had recently? Do you watch a lot of videos (of news, tv, entertainment)? We take on exactly what we surround ourselves with, as much as we try to block it or let it go, it still does affect us.

After the past six months of debates, there's been plenty of videos to watch, plenty of tv, and plenty of entertainment, but thats not all. To feel relief of all the stress, many people have watched enormous amounts of tv, Netflix, hbo and the like. Live streaming has become a huge hit, and many new products have become accessible to us. Ie. amazon fire stick, google chrome cast, apple tv, etc. Having cable tv is not a necessity anymore. However, its not just tv that affects our energy bodies. In addition, we've gone through the Holidays, winter shopping, rekindling with old family members, friends, and had more pressures with work, career, and bills. In addition, maybe you reconnected with an old love, an old flame, or re-established a connection that has been long lost.
All of these things we surround ourselves with, does indeed affect our energy bodies. As you know from reading my blog, our energy body, is a part of our physical body, so anything we experience, get close to, or spend quality time with, will affect the energy we live in, even if our intention is not to have this be so. We are vibrational beings, made up of mostly water and energy, so there's no escaping the energy.

However, we can choose to harness practices to release it.

As soon as you realize this, the important thing is to get back to your meditation, your bathing ritual, a fresh walk outdoors, an energy cleansing, or nice massage. Sometimes its important to remove yourself from the computer or tv for a while and regain your balance and center. What do you do when you realize you've taken on too much energy from your surroundings, and notice, you too have become an "energy magnet"? Where is the source of the energy you have taken on? And, what steps will you take to remove yourself, or "get clean"?

18 Healing with the Chakras
Tantric & Kundalini Awakening

Chanting the names of these chakras (see pictures below) allows the energy to rise and move to the crown (at the top of your head). As this energy rises, after breathing this energy up for several minutes or longer, one can experience a feeling of bliss, energy awakening around your body, tingles and sensations of love and joy within the body, and a feeling of deep relaxation and peace!

Chanting these names sitting in front of your partner, or beloved also allows the two people to experience bliss. When sitting in a Tantric Yab yum position, a couple can experience these sensations together, and can also feel the love of their hearts connecting at a level possibly never experienced before. In tantric history and following a tantric path, when making love in this Yab yum position, love making will never be the same! The breathing, chanting and tantric movements in this position need to be practiced, and without practicing the breathing, chanting and movements in this position, the experience cannot be felt. Couples need to be disciplined in this practice and allow each other to become fully vulnerable in their presence with each other, as this allows them to connect to the divine, and in essence, their true hearts love!

Crown Chakra - 7th Chakra

Third Eye - 6th Chakra

Throat - 5th Chakra

Heart - 4th Chakra

Solar Plexus - 3rd Chakra

Sacral - 2nd Chakra

Root - 1st Chakra

The Sacred sound is Om - Crown Chakra

The Crown Chakra is to open the spiritual center; your expanded connection to the universe, where you feel a oneness to all of life; to all of humanity and all around you. Your Crown Chakra is your true spiritual teacher.
It is the portal to Divine Wisdom and Guidance.

The Sacred sound is Sham - Third Eye Chakra

The third eye to open your inner vision, and your knowledge center, the ability to see the future, and the truth! It helps awaken knowing, true knowing, knowledge and the ability to be grounded and strong in the mind. It is the window to see your soul!

The Sacred sound is Hom - Throat Chakra

The Throat Chakra to open the throat center and your inner voice! It is there to help you release the energy of all other chakras, bring voice and balance to each of them. It is there to expand your power, creativity and truth to the world; feeling fully heard, how you communicate, voice what you feel, and even experience how others hear you.

The Sacred sound is Yam - Heart Chakra

The Heart Chakra to open the heart; the place where compassion resides, releasing the feeling of abandonment, loss, loneliness, sadness, depression, and feeling disconnected to the love others have for you or the love you have for yourself! It is to help you bring awareness back to this love, and bring it back to you!

The Sacred sound is Ram - Solar Plexus Chakra

The Solar Plexus, your third chakra, to open the control center; the central place of anger. The Solar Plexus is to help you forgive, surrender, let go of the need to control and take care always of others, and to balance you when feeling controlled by others! It is there to bring balance to your power center, and be awakened to your inner strength.

The Sacred sound is Vam - Sacral Center Chakra

The Sacral Chakra is your source to heal your old relationships, your creative forces that reside within you and resurface upon clearing. You will access and open your sexuality with this chakra, and find the bliss that hides inside of you!

The Sacred sound is Lam - Root Chakra

The Root Chakra to open your base chakra, your root area; your center of security and stability. The Root Chakra is connected to your relationship to your parents since birth, your relationship to money, grounding your physical body and connecting to Earth.

19 Purifying the Body

The journey to cleansing and purifying oneself is not an easy task, but so worth it.

When I was in high school, I was an avid athlete. I was on the track team every fall, the swim team every winter, the tennis team every spring and had three young brothers to play the role of tom boy with. I also joined the ski team for fun with my high school and our rival school in the same town every year. I rode a mountain bike, played basketball in the driveway, kicked the soccer ball around, threw the football with my brothers, played ping pong with my mom; who was on the team in college herself, and even tried out for field hockey. I loved sports and kept myself very busy as a young woman.

In my early twenties, I discovered I had multiple cavities one after the next. My teeth had lost their protective coating and I had to go to the dentist to get fillings put in. I did not know anything about the content of the fillings; all I knew is that I needed them.

I discovered soon after, my body went into shock and I had muscle knots everywhere and had a hard time walking. I needed pain relievers but had refused to take them. I lived in the bath tub, and with persistence and struggle found myself going to acupuncturists, chiropractors, massage therapists, the hot tub, steam room & sauna. After about 4 years of committing myself to the natural alternatives to pain, I found myself going to school for Acupressure and Massage. The pain is what lead me on the path. The pain lead me to transform myself inside and out.

About 10 years on this journey later, I discovered what the side effects are of amalgam/mercury heavy metal fillings can do to the body. My heart sank. I cried for tears of joy. A conclusion to a struggle I never knew existed.

I have had 2 fillings taken out and replaced with a healthier alternative so far. The 2nd one I had replaced only one week ago. My body has been a little tired going through a detox, but already I notice a difference. I can carry my son from the car to inside, and I haven't felt the throbbing pain that usually causes me to put him down in a hurry. I can jump into warrior pose without feeling the need to breathe through the pain. A couple days ago, my son ran to me in a sprint, and I picked him up over my head and spun him around, about 4 times in a row. I felt no discomfort. I did, however, feel a little tired. From these small examples, I am super excited, as I know only progress will continue. Soon I'll be doing forward flips off a diving board and on a mat. Oh, I forgot to tell you, I used to be a gymnast. This was one of my favorite things to do. Other benefits of this will be that I'll be able to give much longer and deeper massages, and most likely more often! Only time will tell, but the patience to get where I am now has been well worth it!

Blessings to life!

20 Awakening Passion With Art

Sometimes when inspiration calls, and there is no time for being alone or with a loved one, one way of expressing yourself is through the arts. And, in my experience, being with my little one, alone in our home, I took to my paint markers. And, in the process I found myself feeling excited for having completed a piece of art, even better that it was starting to look beautiful, and even more so that I did it myself and completed the task at hand.

Art is an excellent tool used for healing and there is a unique therapy specialized in Psychotherapy where some become trained as Art Therapists. I find myself drawn so deeply to Art Therapy and when I am in need of expressing my own passion, and I have a toddler running around to take care of and absolutely no privacy of my own, I like to fall to writing and in today's case, my beautiful paint markers.

I love painting and have not done so in a long time, but it brings up the reminder of how much I love this and brings me in touch with the feelings of excitement and fulfillment just for having done a piece of art. Art in itself is therapeutic to the mind, soothing to the emotions and meditative to the spirit. As much as I can, I'm going to take the rest of today immersed back in my vibrant colors and put my creative passions to use. And, in the process I feel my own passion and excitement for life come back alive, and be filled with expression to another level again!

21 Kundalini Orgasmic Meditation

Intention: A gentle meditation practice incorporating breathing into the belly and expanding the breath throughout the entire body. Orgasmic Meditation helps to ignite pleasure in the body, feel peace, but also bliss. It is a guided meditation to channel sexual energy throughout the body, clear energy, and raise sexual and spiritual energy.

Grounding and Shielding: You will find yourself a seat in the room, choosing to sit upright or laying down on a pillow or blanket. You will start with breathing into the belly, breathing in the nose and out the mouth. Feel your connection to the earth, but also your body and the energy around you. Notice the frequency in your energy field. Get present to how you feel, and breathe that knowing into your belly, exhaling out the mouth to release any stress you feel.

Balancing: As you feel deeper into your body and feel more comfortable with your breathing, you will start to inhale in through the top of the head, and exhale the breath down the legs.

Intention and Declaration: Whatever intention you have is for your personal awareness. Examples are: love myself deeper, love my partner deeper, clear myself of stress, remove stagnation or armor, open my heart more for giving and receiving love, gain the ability to make love longer, etc.

Completion and Grounding: As you go deeper into your breathing process, you will forget you are sitting in a room with other people, you will enjoy the pleasure of your breath, and appreciate your body more. You may have a mini full body energetic orgasm. This can be a short practice or a long practice. However, you will gain a taste of the possibilities this provides, and if your energy is open, receive incredible joy from the process. As we come to a close you will breathe slower, longer, and more gently, exhaling into the earth to connect, get settled, and ground.

This is not a chakra meditation practice, but a kundalini meditation to help bring opening throughout the chakra channel, removing blocks along the central pathway of the body, and inhaling to increase the sexual energy flow, and exhaling by bringing the sexual energy down to ground.

It helps to bring awareness to how open your energy is, and also is a practice that can be learned to do on your own. It helps with erectile dysfunction, healing the prostate, elongating your love making experience and strengthening your sexual muscles for health, pleasure and multiple orgasms. Great for men and women!

Asttarte Deva Shakti Bliss

**Section 2
Tantra Yoga**

22

Unveiling the Eyes

Philadelphia is filled with people who are armored, on the defense, ready to attack or always in fear that they themselves will be. Out of everywhere in the world, where we reside, in Philadelphia, is known to be the angriest, hostile and scared human beings. The theme is success, wealth and looking good. Most are open to yoga and know of it, as it is a practice that many think is strictly about toning the body and getting in shape. However, there are other levels to yoga that are not as known. Yoga offers healing that can open the heart at a level no other physical exercise can offer.

When people cross by each other on the street, there are very few who will take the time to look into your eyes; even fewer smile out of courtesy to be polite. It is a rare occasion that someone driving will wait for you as you pull your car out of a spot or slowly get into your spot while you attempt to parallel park. Many are impatient, rude, always rushing, in a hurry to get to x, y, and z; often not even knowing why they are in such a hurry.

In the practice of eye gazing, there is a window of opportunity that allows you to be met with love, creating intimacy with another just for the pure innocence of loving. Like the affection from a mother caressing her baby with love as she gazes at her child; that feeling of being in love with your baby that a parent often feels is the same unconditional love that can be created through eye gazing.

As you look into another's eyes, and are met with the same persistent gaze of commitment as the person looking at you, the wall of defense, the armor that our eyes can sometimes live in, is given an opportunity to melt away. The eyes are the window to the soul, and I like to view them as an extension of the heart. As you sit in the eye gazing meditation with another, the tears of armor has a chance to be revealed, released and dropped away. Literally tears can sometimes arrive; not as a sign of weakness that you have sadness, but rather, a courage that you are willing to be seen and hold presence for or from another, and the tears symbolize that armoring falling away. As the armor falls away, from our eyes, from our hearts, a deeper connection of intimacy has a chance to be created; a feeling of safety, of love, of beauty, of pure connection to another. Only through being vulnerable and allowing oneself to be seen, be met, be grounded in anchoring your heart to the earth with the connection to another is the opportunity for deep connection of intimacy allowed to be manifest.

So love, let your love in, let others love you, and open yourself to allowing the truth of your heart to give to others in love. There is no greater gift on this planet than love. It is what everyone desires!

23 Thoughts on Tantra

Letter to a friend:

Tantra is about being with the moment - not judging negative emotions as something bad, or wrong or being afraid them, but rather using them as tools to go deeper into the psyche, the unconscious, to create more love and presence in the moment to what is. While in the presence of your beloved, as you see she is perhaps angry or sad, instead of yelling at her or being upset that she is angry or sad, just letting her be sad, letting her be mad, and being a witness, loving her through her pain, so the pain can eventually depart - release and let go - by having been present to the pain, holding consciousness to it, accepting it, allowing it to be heard, seen, and accepted will ultimately allow it to leave. This then will allow the other to trust, feel loved, and feel a deeper connection to herself, to you and to everything all around her.

Just like when you go to get a massage, the MT does not force the muscles to relax and release the tightness. The MT holds loving presence to the pain, the tightness, the area where the body is holding stress - and as this area is accepted as it is, knows it is loved, it can feel the ability to expand itself, and in that expansion, it can be vulnerable, release what it was holding onto, and let it go, and then the tightness, the pain, surrenders and releases.

A book you might like is called The Joy of Feeling, by Iona Marsaa Teegarden. It is from my Jin Shin Do Bodymind Acupressure training, and has a lot of Psychotherapy, Taoism, Chi, Energy Psychology, and methods for releasing trauma, pain and deep held emotions. It is not a book on tantra, but this is the basis for tantra. It's a way of using Body-Mind Consciousness to empower, grow, and heal.

Yes, I know that the journey of life is not about always healing, but when things come up, and you can be a witness to them, it allows the patterns to change, so the dynamic and magnetism to unhealthy situations clear their layers and more loving situations, experiences, and people are then drawn to you.

Having been raped as a child, and again as an adult, I would not have healed or recovered by controlling my feelings, but instead letting myself feel whatever it is, so I can shift into deeper love - of love, forgiveness and acceptance to everything that has happened to me and live a life of love through transforming the darkness that happened before. Transforming the present allows the past to be transformed as well, and connection to the divine just happens. As I allow myself to be who I really am, the real me underneath the outer shell can be revealed and be free! And every moment is an opportunity to allow that freedom to be experienced!

We all have had stress in our lives, and in our childhood that stress carries over into our adulthood, the relationships with our friends, lovers and co-workers, and as you suppress your feelings only more pain manifests, but as you allow the pain in the present to be revealed through loving presence, all the pain from the past can be transformed as well.

Perhaps we have similar goals, but the journey to getting there is just different, or the description has different words, but the love in the end is the same!

Another book you might like is called: The Wisdom of Listening, or any book by David Deida or Osho.

24 Tantra is Not the easy path

For those of you who are looking for an easy fix or an easy way out, you will not find it with tantra. If you want to run away from your problems, or escape into a fairy land place where everything disappears, and all your daily struggles go away, you will not find that with tantra. Some people want the easy life. They don't want to have to work. They don't want to have grow, or go deep into themselves to work out their own problems and find a solution. They would just rather not do anything at all. As you know, from my recent partner, this was his way of working things out; by not working them out. Being a Dakini and a Tantra Practitioner, there was a difference in beliefs.

The Tantric path is about going as deep as you can possibly go until you find the answer, instead of the former, not looking at all for any answers and walking away. I am here to help others transform themselves to move into light and find the love that is missing inside, and in order to find that love, one must dig to get there, and doing nothing resolves nothing. Doing nothing, creates a situation where disconnections happen, walls are built, resistances are created, the mystery of silence then forms, and the relationship turns into a dark hole where there is nowhere to go and no way of getting out. The only solution left then is to walk away and find love once again.

When you embark on a path of tantra, you have to be willing to face all of yourself; your fears, worries, concerns, resentments, patterns and look at the dark side of yourself. This is the only way to then turn yourself back into light. When the person you love or you yourself do not want to look at what is causing you pain, then the pain stays inside you and it is only you then who is causing it, and no one else. No one can heal without the desire to look at their own wounds, and in whatever form they are in, the best solution is to shed light on them, so they can then be given permission to leave.

Through tantra, all of the dark sides of ourselves are given permission to leave, from being awoken to the surface, being given the opportunity to express itself, be heard, loved, and ultimately then surrender and allowed to leave. Without presence to anything painful, it only stays inside, hidden, unknown, and afraid. This can reflect someone's relationships, their health, their career, their family, their friendships, their free time, and their freedom within their own lives. Transformation in any area of life, can be created through tantra, and given the opportunity and expression to be free!

25 Tantra Yoga on the mat

In my Tantra Yoga Sessions, it is just like going to a Yoga class. Everyone is at a different level in their development in Tantra Yoga and there is no competition to be something greater, or different than you already are, because where you are, is exactly the way you are supposed to be. Your desire and intention in doing Tantra Yoga and starting a practice of learning what is possible for your life, is the biggest acknowledgment and honor you could give yourself. Just allow yourself to experience what you are going to experience. Surrender to where you are in your life and who you are as a person. Tantra Yoga has almost the same principles as Yoga, and the best way to be is a witness to yourself and to accept yourself fully for the mat you are on, because your life is exactly the way its supposed to be right now. If it were any different, you wouldn't be you!

26 The Psychology of Tantra

Being Real, Authentic and you!

Who is the real you? What is the real you? When you can sit back and let yourself be open, expressive, engaging and not have to think about what you say, or how you act, and can let go without thinking in advance, you can be alive and true to the real self you are. It's not always easy to let one's guard down, and scream when you feel like it, or cry as soon as you notice you are sad, and the sadness comes from an ancient feeling held tight inside of you. Being authentic and true to one's self, by means of expression is a gift and ability not many are able to live, and seldom even allow themselves the freedom to know it's power and believe it is even possible.

What does it mean to release one's hidden emotions? What does it mean to hold on tight to all your feelings inside? Why is this of any value or have any significance to one's living?

Because these actions and feelings can create power! The power is created when you let go of anything you've been hanging onto from your ancient past, or recent problems. When you hold on to an old feeling, knowing that it is inside, and how strong you've been holding onto it and how much pain it has caused you, you know the holding on is creating as much strength and power in the emotion and feeling as it would if you were to let it go. Holding onto something gives it power. Putting thought to an idea, or a feeling gives it power. And, when you know it is still there, and how difficult it is to even think about, this alone gives this feeling such power over your entire way of living, being, looking at life, and ability to respond to something. The same power and strength is given back to you, when you can finally make peace with the feeling, bring light to it, show the feeling it is loved, being able to look straight on to this emotion and surrendering to all it's pains, also can create power by loving yourself in the emotion/feeling/behavior/held emotion from the past, that you can become empowered and enlightened just from setting this feeling free!

So, when you can let go of a painful truth, shed its tears, or let it have a temper tantrum and scream and jump up and down until it feels heard, you can finally be free of this feeling, have a stronger ability to be present in the moment, feel heard, known, accepted and loved, then you can truly be your authentic you!

27 Tantra As Self Empowerment

There are many sayings in times past on "reclaiming your power", or "Women Power", or finding empowerment through sports or martial arts. Few ever talk about, and even fewer know about the hidden secrets and power within Tantra. Tantra as empowerment is a way of reclaiming oneself, finding out who you are, learning tools to access who you are, and then practicing the Tantra techniques, exercises and practices. Tantra allows one a way of manifesting the life you want - the abundance you seek, the lover or beloved of your dreams, the harmonious and passionate relationship and love life you desire with the one you already have, the car or house of your dreams, and so on.

Tantra is empowering because it forces you to tap into your will and draw up energies within yourself to go beyond the uncomfortable until eventually it does become comfortable. I have found no other writings or research on Tantra as self-empowerment, but this is one of the biggest reasons ancient masters studied and practiced, and also taught this powerful practice.

Tantra is Yoga; however, Yoga is not Tantra. Tantra forces one to become present to the pain within themselves as well as is open to one becoming present, at one and authentic to the joy and blissful nature of oneself. Tantra is about being open to what is. Yoga is about being a Warrior and controlling ones urges to just be still and allow the energies of feelings to move through them, while Tantra teaches one to embrace, be open and be real with those feelings; authenticity, however, done with presence, listening to the breath, and the still voice within. I love Tantra Yoga because it teaches me about the natural desires of the human nature and about being real and accepting of them, and using that realness within oneself as a vehicle to grow; by accepting what is.

Tantra as self-empowerment is as natural as following your bliss and listening to that inner voice inside yourself of what you should or shouldn't do. It is also about doing a set of exercises to harness the deep emotions within yourself, so you can eventually pull them up and out of you, and let them go; be them rage, anger, sadness, confusion, numbness or fear.

Whatever the emotion, Tantra gives you a vehicle to transcend them. And that alone is empowering. And that alone allows anyone, anywhere to give birth to a new life; one of bliss, joy, contentedness and peace. This is why I call Tantra a miracle. This is why I call Tantra self-empowering. This is why Tantra can be used as a tool for Psychotherapy, and this is why Tantra is a gift from God.

28 Remembering Presence

During the moments of quiet within each breath and the whispers of every second, remaining still becomes presence, and holding space is all that is. As I sit and hold space for my clients, I remember how tranquil and beautiful it feels to be still and present. And in time in sessions this beauty and presence feels like it could last for eternity. Being present is a meditation and a joy to achieve, and although it sounds simple to attain, for many it can be very difficult. And so, this is where tantra practice comes in to achieve this balance and doing this with another allows the attainment that much easier. Offering the sessions to another allows the mirror to be reflected; the love you put out comes back to you, the peace you put out comes back to you, and the presence you put out comes back you. Anything you give is received and offered back as love. And so, in being still, we create this miracle together.

It has been a couple months since I've offered sessions from after the birth of my beautiful baby. As I return to my practice and the sacred art of healing, by giving of service through sessions, I return to what I love and remember the beauty of being still. As I give to others, I also receive and in teaching meditation and love to others, I also reach the still place of meditation and love in my own self. This gift of giving can be a miracle; not only the miracle of healing to others, but also the miracle of healing oneself.

I only know the depth and immensity of what healing can do for others by how deep it has impacted my own life. My own testimony to how much I have transformed from all healing paths that I have been trained, received healing, and have had experience in some way is the only way that I know how intensely powerful they all are. However, you must be truly willing to delve deep inside in order to come out of your own shell like the butterfly blossoms from its cocoon.

As we become still in moments that feel challenging to slow down our body, and slow down our mind, this is when we can truly transform and open our hearts to a more serene place of love. And in being present to others we are also present to ourselves. And, in Tantra, this is healing in a universal way; helping the self and helping the other as the circle of energy makes its way around; from you into them, from them into you and continues this cycle again and again until you choose to end the practice. The energy cycles and circulates from one to another and presence remains while love grows stronger and healing blossoms from within. There is nothing more beautiful and miraculous than this. Slowing down is the biggest key to healing; whether it is tantric healing or any other form; practicing presence is all you need.

29 Hug Therapy

"Hugs are innocent, natural, fun and Healing! Everyone needs a hug, but an extended hug from a Tantra Practitioner, offers a world of opportunities!"

Hug Therapy can open many possibilities in yourself and in your life. It can help lift a weight of stress on your entire body, release energy blocks, slowly awaken a heart that was once closed, and allow for healing any emotions that are at the surface and ready to be released. It can also fulfill a deep need to be touched, nurtured or supported by the simple act of affection of a hug. This practice can help you learn how to breathe deeply, so as to allow the hug in and you begin to feel safe in allowing yourself to be loved, as well as feel safe in allowing yourself to love another; the act of giving and receiving balances yourself to what had blocked you from offering yourself, or being taken care of before. The act of Hugging over an extended period of time creates feelings in oneself that you are deserving, worth being loved, and helps you to remember that you are completely capable of loving another.

Hug Therapy is a very powerful experience, especially when done by someone who accepts you unconditionally. Like a therapist who loves you and supports you no matter what you are going through; as a Tantra Practitioner, my heart is open to loving you, and allowing whatever feelings that come up to be supported and nurtured in the moment. Hug Therapy also opens blocks in your ability to fully express yourself, communicate what you have kept secret, gives you the ability to trust your feelings that what matters to you is truly important, and your ability in expressing yourself through whatever way matters to you; art, writing, singing, dancing, intimacy, sex, etc. is allowed to be released and let free once again!

30 What is the meaning of Tantra & Tantra Massage?

What is Tantra really? Everyone has their own idea of what tantra is, honestly. People overuse it, and yet, it is not truly understood. Tantra is a spiritual practice derived from ancient yoga traditions, as well as Buddhist, Hindu, and Egyptian. Where did it really come from? No one really knows. Some people believe the spiritual teachings of the planet came from the Atlanteans and Pleidians, and perhaps from another planet, a faraway galaxy, that came to visit our beloved Earth and give us teachings to help the future, which is in fact, today!

Tantra is a practice of bridging consciousness, presence, the breath, honoring the energy of oneself, one's essence of life force, and healing, and connecting it with the place within we all strive to connect to; our hearts, our ability to feel love, loving another, receiving as well as giving love outside of ourselves. One would associate tantra with Yoga because yoga is a practice of the breath, however, many traditional yoga practices excludes the honoring of one's natural innate abilities to feel all of oneself, feel love for oneself, and love for another. So, yoga is not all. Yoga is limiting. Tantra does not limit the whole self. Tantra includes all of the self; the whole being, the whole body, the whole breath, the whole spirit, the whole universe, and the oneness around each and every one of you, as well as feeling into all that which is inside of yourself.

Many Yoga practices focus on asana poses, pranayama, breathing, the chakras, the soul, simple meditation, as well as mantra, Sanskrit words of prayer, mudras, stillness, and the kundalini energy. However, because the classics of yoga want to keep the tradition of yoga on the spiritual essence of the soul, they eliminate the fullness of the capacity to feel all of one's self and one's body. It believes in a strong structure, and boundaries of the self, and keeps a wall up around the idea of connection, intimacy and love. That is the only missing link between traditional yoga and tantra yoga. However, tantra yoga can go beyond the simple idea of intimacy, connection and love, and go to its greatest heights of connection and be boundary-less. This is where each individual needs to instill their own boundaries, and their own rules, and hence, the main reason why *every* person has a different definition as to what tantra really means.

Tantra Massage

Why all the hype about Tantra Massage? Why is it such a main topic of interest, focus, and what's the big idea anyway? Well, thoughts create reality, and if the majority of society think that tantra equals sex, then they believe that is what it is. However, tantra *does not* equal sex. In fact, love does not always equal sex, nor does intimacy. Sex means sex. Love means love. And tantra means tantra. Bottom line. There are often and sometimes crossovers, however, they do not mean the same thing. Now, often, massage can induce feelings of sensuality, however, massage is a separate practice. It is mainly created for relaxation, healing of the muscles, and opening of the cells and energy of one's body. Sometimes, opening these channels creates an opening in ones feeling center to desire more of a sensual touch, or feeling a connection to the deeper emotions inside their heart, which is the love for themselves, as well as their ability to feel love for another. However, sensual feelings are not love. Love is love, and often it has to do with the feeling for oneself, or someone they feel deep inside their heart. There is a crossover of feeling a moment of love, bliss and peace to feeling a deep heartfelt connection of love for someone they truly care for. These can be defined very differently depending on what love means to each individual. Often love cannot be defined. Often, many people feel love very easily, especially when one loves themselves and is capable of feeling deep love and peace for others. However, if someone has a lot of trauma and unable to feel deep love for themselves, they clearly won't be able to feel love for anyone else either, or perhaps not easily. Or, their idea of love may be threatened, challenged, and they will feel defensive about their definition of love, how they choose to define it, and explain in any length what intimacy means to them. So, perhaps, they won't be able to understand what tantra is, if they don't really know what love is, and intimacy causes many triggers, and fears that dwell up inside themselves.

So, what in fact is tantra massage? Well, it's what each individual needs to feel a deep love for themselves; bottom line. It's not about feeling a love for the person outside of them, whoever it might be giving them the massage. It's about how to unravel the walls that are guarding the person to feel a deep bliss, peacefulness, expansion of their own chakras to connect to the kundalini, heart opening for themselves, and experience a full body bliss, that could be experienced as pleasure, or simply a full body feeling of love.

31 Tantra After the Holidays

What are you doing to keep yourself feeling sexy and loved? How are you getting the connection and intimacy you desire? Are you still getting your needs met after the peak of the holidays? The middle of the holidays often can be a celebration and healing of love with family, and especially your partner, husband or wife. It may be a chance you can spend more time together, with work days off, more family members helping out with your kids, or a chance to just be home alone. When that joy of the holidays and opportunity to spend together is over, how do you keep the sparkle going?

Perhaps you went away together to a foreign country like Spain, or Greece, or a ski country like Australia, or Alaska. Did you snuggle up to the fire after hours of feeling the wind rush on your face, and massage each other after landing at the bottom of the hill as you pounded the ground and watched the snow fly in the air using all your thighs and strength of your Gluteus Maxima, minima, posterior and interior muscles?

Rekindling the flame after an intense connection and Holiday season can sometimes be challenging when you are a hard worker and have a successful business or career. Perhaps one way of keeping the connection going is to go to a Tantra Retreat, workshop or a weekend getaway somewhere local. A night out on the town, and back to a hotel room with a jacuzzi tub sounds delightful.

Sometimes even just a simple practice of meditation together can ignite the fire, and remove the energy and stress of work and everyday life. It can help to cleanse the energy and let the kundalini sexual energy rise again, especially between two people who originally had an intense and powerful connection. It will always come back after a little cleansing. If you have not been on a meditation practice, perhaps consider the opportunity there for igniting a tantric connection. It's simple and free.

Did you have a good holiday, and now you feel distant from your loved one again? Consider planning something with the one you love the most. And, if you already feel close to him or her that you love, do something to celebrate!

I celebrate with you in your passion and love, and hope for it to continue as long as you desire!

32 Tantra and Patience

Bringing patience into your experience of tantra, and your deep love for yourself, the healing process you are going through, as well as meeting your beloved where he or she is, and allowing the unfolding to happen is a gradual process. Removing the pressure on yourself for your own journey of healing, and knowing you will expand, unravel and heal when you do, in your own time, is a perfect blend of giving patience to your partner, and allowing him or her to go through what they need to, in their time, and come back to you, to your heart and love you when they are ready. It will strengthen your love for yourself when you can be patient with yourself, not judging yourself for where you are, and when you can be patient with yourself, you can also be patient with the partner you love as well.

Many people try to rush to get to some conclusion, some destination, and think that once they arrive, they will "finally" be happy. It's not about the destination in life, however. We see it all over in slogans around the world, like a sort of trademark, "It's not about the destination. It's the journey that counts." The journey is where you learn your life lessons, where you learn who you are, what you need, your greatest discoveries. The journey is the path you need to be patient with yourself and others, and it's the path you learn to truly love yourself, and in doing so, the ability to love everyone around you as well.

When you can find acceptance in the moment, in yourself, in your journey, and acceptance in where others are at, what they are experiencing, how they unfold, how they understand, you can give them the love that they perhaps don't know how to give themselves.

When it comes to both Tantra and Patience, as in the title of this section, I am speaking here about taking all the time you need for you, and in doing so, letting others do the same. Being patient with yourself, is not an easy task, when you've lived a long life of feeling competitive, being a leader, being a provider, having others rely on you, or feeling pressured to do everything right, doing it perfect, getting all your needs met by a certain time, having expectations put upon by yourself or by others, and doing it promptly. We all learn to put pressure on ourselves. But Tantra is a path of patience. It's a Yoga practice, so one must learn to surrender in the moment, to themselves, to how they are feeling, and learn to listen, be humble and humbled with others. It's a path of the breath, of slowing down the breath, a path of learning to listen, to the still small voice within, to the still sounds within, how you feel within, and doing it so profoundly that you can do this for others as well.

If you have an infection, or a serious illness, there is no rushing it. You must give your body, mind and spirit the time it takes to process the illness or infection through your system. All your bodies processors must go through the slow subtle changes, allowing each cell to move to the next stage, and expand until it reaches maturity, its heightened capacity of climax, and then slowly unravel to its ability to simmer down, distill out of each area, and surrender into oneself, relaxing, gently coming to a place of calm, integration, and eventually moving to the end of its cycle where one is fully healed and recovered. This all takes time and is a journey of the deeper cells, bacteria, and inner alchemy of one's own bodies. Every human body processes these molecular and chemical changes in its own time, and its own journey. When you are out sick, and you call your boss to tell him, you need to stay home, he doesn't say, "Well hurry up, and get well, and get rid of your damn illness. You're not supposed to be sick anyway. I need you here today." He is, hopefully instead, understanding, and gives you the time you need to rest, and eventually recover.

As a survivor of a long-term illness myself, I know the journey of healing and being patient is crucial in coming to acceptance and letting your body do what it needs to do to feel better. Some illnesses never go away. But many, with the right treatment, love, knowledge and research, and time put into the process of healing, do eventually come to a place of health.

Your love for yourself has to harness the same degree of patience, as well as your love for your deeply beloved. You cannot give up on someone you love, when you know they are going through something incredibly challenging. That is the exact time they need you the most! You must not judge them, but love them. You must not criticize them for how they feel, but love them. You must not disappear on them, or distance yourself when they are going through something, but love them. When you run away from someone you love, you are also running away from yourself.

When your partner is going through a process of healing, it's important to do your own self-reflection and healing, and if what they say, and are going through causes you to have a reaction, to also look at your own experience, feelings, and what causes you to feel as you do. Your partners experience is separate and distinct from your own. Each individual has their own journey, their own reactions, feelings, emotions, and sensations that cause them to feel a certain way. When you can take responsibility for your feelings, and your partner can take responsibility for his or hers, you both win!

33 Tantra Is Life; The Misconception of the "word" Tantra

Tantra is life, it is nothing short of everything you see, everything you feel and everything you experience.

Tantra is the warm rush of water from your shower as you roll your back from side to side to breathe in its gifts of pleasure, and exhaling sighs of relief.

Tantra is the experience you have, lying in your bed upon waking, and noticing the feelings that surfaced from a dream you just had, and your desire to lay there and feel all of it, remembering the dream, and running through it in your head, feeling its joy, its sadness, its teaching inside your cells. And allowing yourself to experience those feelings.

Tantra is the feeling you have when you comfort your pet, holding him or her, sitting in the silence, and breathing in the peace and love of stillness in the moment, and perhaps feeling the love and cherishing it.

Tantra is the utter joy when you walk in a room, and smell the delicious scent of cookies you love (or any food you love), and breathe in the memories it gives you, and feeling the joy not only from the smell, but also the memory inside your body.

Tantra is the utter euphoria you feel when you look at a horizon and take in its beauty, or when gazing at a huge garden of flowers, or an aggressive water fall running over a mountain, down a river, or at the edge of a cliff, or when you gaze upon a couple and notice their depth of love for one another, the innocent smile of a baby, a beautiful row of trees, a field of endless grass, the far reaching waters miles into the ocean, or any image that you deem miraculous or beautiful!

It is when you pause while walking, and notice a pain in your muscle, and stop to feel it, take a breath, experience it deeper, and continue walking to your destination.

It is when someone lovingly touches your hand, or your shoulder in an offer of kindness.

It is when you go to a place of memory from the past, and you notice your heart flutter, and a rush of energy flows through you, perhaps even tears rise to your eyes.

It is when you walk on the land, on the dirt, on rocks, and you notice pleasure run all the way through your body, a body orgasm, and the biggest smile runs across your face. And you don't need to explain it. You just feel it, and are still, yet chills of joy are vibrating through you.

It is when you take a taste of food, something so delicious and magical, that you pause, breathe in and exhale moans of joy.

It is the sensation when connected with your lover, or partner, whilst making love, or after, and feel their utter depth of love for you, or you feel your utter depth of love for them, and your heart melts, and you melt into each other, and you feel it in all your cells, your muscles, your bones, your energy, your heart and your soul. And you have no desire to go anywhere, but be still, and hold each other in your love.

Tantra is that blissful feeling you have when you're looking at the person you love, and you feel joy in your body when you know you're about to embrace them in your arms!

Tantra is the feeling of stillness, peace, joy, presence and oneness in everything you think, feel and do. It is all that is! It is consciousness arising!

Tantra is love, it is gentle, it is sweet, it is kind!

34 What Tantra is Not

After learning what tantra is, you may know what tantra is not, however, what I am going to explain what tantra is not, is not believable to many. So, I'm going to elaborate on what this means here.

Tantra is not erotica. Tantra is not sex. It is not a practice of porn or sexual gratification. Tantra is not for the simple minded, the superficial, or purely physical. Tantra is not a practice of quick connection or intimacy.

Erotica is a very provocative art and literature to arouse sexual desire. Many merge tantra with sexual art, because it can be viewed as something very beautiful, very sensual, and depict images of lovers embracing in intimacy, deep sexual pleasure and love. However, tantra by itself, is not erotica. When two lovers come together, are deeply in love, married, or have moments of embrace, and are viewed by the public eye, such as in images, pictures, paintings, or drawings, it certainly has the element of erotica. The distinction is in the connection between the lovers, their level of relationship, closeness, or harmony together. When it is two strangers, coming together for modeling to an artist, a writer, a videographer, or screenwriter, it can certainly be seen as erotica.

Sex is purely a physical act. It is the act of making love, however, completely of the physical element. It is when two people engage in full connection and boundary-less interactions. With tantra, there are boundaries. There does not have to include sexual activity, however, it may, but sex by itself excludes the spiritual and emotional component. There are many rules to tantra when it comes to a practice of engaging in connection with another human being. Sex by itself does not often include rules, however, when incorporating another individual's feelings around sex, what sex means to them, what they need, are comfortable or are uncomfortable with, yes, there can be certain rules to how to connect with your lover.

Tantra is not porn or sexual gratification. Porn is certainly something people watch to observe others in engaging in sexual activity, and sexual gratification is certainly what people seek out to get rid of, and remove a feeling of frustration of pent up energy they often don't get rid of, mostly from being single, but also from being in a relationship that has a lot of walls, barriers to intimacy, communication blocks, time lapses between connecting, and issues keeping the connection, love, and sexual involvement at a strong low or dismissed all together. Sexual gratification is something people look for to help them feel an urgent and rushed closeness to another human being, release a sexual frustration, but it doesn't include a pure closeness of love or tantric love. It excludes tantra. It is purely sexual in nature.

Tantra does not rush. It does not ignore feelings, or energies in the moment. Tantra does not create instant results.

Tantra purely IS love, gentle, slow, relaxed intimacy, healing of the entire self, and the opposite of rushing or gratification. It often does include sexual connection; however, it also is done very *very* lovingly and slow. It adds an element of presence to sex.

35 The Sacred Arts: The Different Shades of Tantra

When no one has had any background in White Tantra, or Spiritual Discipline practices, we start there before we move to other types of tantra. Many people have little background in spirituality, the breath, energy work, or yoga and need a lot of healing, so wherever the person needs the attention, focus, healing and area to address, we will start there. Often, the aspirant/student is not the one who has awareness of what he needs. Often, the individual is too close to his own self to have awareness of what he or she needs to work on, their patterns, issues, and armoring. The practitioner often will know what he/she needs and in order to gain the most benefit and grow the most, one must surrender to that knowledge; In order for foundation of healing and Tantra to begin and grow to a place of consistency, knowledge and commitment.

The Sacred Arts: The Different Shades of Tantra

Expecting to get all your needs met, your relationship fixed and resolved, your sexual energy to rise off the charts, and your energy flowing like the wind? Not all levels of Tantra are the same. Let's take a look at each one, and see what area you need to focus on today. Here are the 5 paths of Tantra to get your energy flowing.

Tantra is becoming very popular here in the West. However, Tantra has been around for thousands of years and continues to evolve as Eastern philosophy and Yoga enter Western psychology, Western Medicine and Western Culture. **Allow me to elaborate to you the different types of Tantra to begin your understanding of the value of beginning where you are right now.** I will describe 5 paths of Tantra. Each path is represented by a color. Within these five tantric paths, there are easily other variations or shades of interpretation available, which would give you the well-known shades of Tantra.

White Tantra is used to describe a spiritual path of Tantra which incorporates meditation, breath work, mantra, sounds and postures. White Tantra incorporates a spiritual practice, to help cleanse the energy body, chakras, the auric field, and begin to awaken one's consciousness of their own innate access to the kundalini that lies dormant within ones being. When the kundalini begins to open, the energy that was hidden will begin to surface, and the emotions that lay hidden there awaken as well. The chakras of a human being begin to awaken, as you start your own spiritual practice of meditation to these areas. The kundalini and the chakras are inter-connected; however, they are not the same thing.

White Tantra also has a component of a physical practice that includes asanas, which is the popular yoga practice of today, hand mudras, similar to sign language, and mantras one uses with a mala, their fingers, or a counter of some sort.

White Tantra also has a correlation to psychotherapy, where as one goes deep into their emotional process, of deep healing in their soul, their inner childhood, their past pains, traumas, fears, angers, upsets, sadness, and more. As the mind opens and clears these past vibrations, the mind begins to open and expand to a new level of awareness. One feels a lightness within, a freshness of spirit, a calmer demeanor, and a greater joy for living, and comfort within one's own body.

As one does their "Tantra" practice, they get attuned to the frequencies that open them up to a higher dimension. It begins to open their heart, and they feel a greater love for the self, as well as a greater love for others. However, with white Tantra, the healing of the self is the priority, and one cannot connect to another before they open up the deeper layers hidden within for their own connection to their deeper self.

White Tantra works on the layers of the energy body around the physical self, and as one does their meditation practice, they awaken their kundalini, and their inner sexual energy arises. This inner sexual energy is where many people confuse Tantra with sex. However, the spiritual practice of Tantra, and the physical act of sex, are two very different things.

The spiritual practice of Tantra is where ones' energy centers connect with our intuitive senses and spirituality. In this culture we tend to equate Tantra with sex. However, the *white Tantra* path doesn't focus on the physical act of sex at all! *White Tantra* is mostly a solo practice between you and spirit. However, just because *White Tantra* is a solo practice, it doesn't mean you can't do your spiritual practice sitting near, close to, or in unison with your partner. However, when your energies open and you choose to do your Tantra practices in connection with your partner, this then is where the *White Tantra* shifts to Pink Tantra.

I personally define Tantra as more of a lifestyle than a religion. However, I recognize that there are some people who practice Tantra as a religion. Some forms of Tantra have become so interlinked with the beliefs of a specific religion such as; Hinduism, Taoism, Buddhism or even Paganism that it is difficult to sort out where Tantra begins and where the religion ends. Within the practice of *White Tantra*, sexual energy is often channeled towards spiritual transformation, personal growth, healing, expanded awareness, and what some might refer to as enlightenment. Sexual activity is not strictly "forbidden" by most of the *White Tantra* practices; however, often devoted followers of *White Tantra* are influenced by religious teachings that value sexual abstinence or celibacy.

If you are an individual who is seeking a journey of spiritual enlightenment or a deeper connection with God or spirit, then perhaps *White Tantra* is an amazing place to be! Kundalini Yoga is a popular practice in this culture that is often categorized as *White Tantra*, however, they are not the same thing. If your reason for exploring tantra is primarily in hopes of learning new ways to improve your sex life, you will need to learn *White Tantra*, before you can move on to studying and practicing pink, red or the other types.

Pink Tantra is a great path to follow when you're in a relationship. It's a practice you can do with your partner, and the main focus is on the heart chakra. Healing your heart chakra helps open one up to the love for the self, as well as gain the ability to love others. It helps heal deeper emotions at the heart center, and as one works on this emotional process, it then impacts all other energy centers of the body.

Pink Tantra refers to a heart centered path of tantra that blends many of the elements of White Tantra into the realm of intimate relationship, excluding the sexual piece of relationships and intimacy.

Within the path of *Pink Tantra*, all of the chakras are acknowledged, however, there is an emphasis on the opening of the heart chakra and healing the heart. The heart chakra has to do with loss, abandonment, grief, sadness, depression, as well as compassion, acceptance, and forgiveness of self as well as others. Pink Tantra teaches us to cultivate love and to learn to surrender, as well as let go of potential expectations, projections and needs of the self or other. With *Pink Tantra* love is seen as the main target for healing and transformation.

Pink Tantra is excellent practice if you're struggling with your current relationship. It provides techniques and practices to help you heal from past relationships, it helps improve your overall feeling of an emotionally balanced life and to connect with your true oneness with self. *Pink Tantra* recognizes the importance of polarity between masculine and feminine energy, yin and yang, as well as inner and outer energies. Practicing *Pink Tantra* will often result in attracting a good potential mate who complements and resonates with your energy. If you are already in a love relationship, this practice will significantly deepen and strengthen your partnership. If your relationship had been struggling, you may experience a rekindling of an emotional and passionate connection with your partner, and a deeper connection of the heart with one another. However, this practice encourages personal wholeness. Sometimes this practice will enable someone to leave a partner who is unhealthy, or otherwise keeping them from being an authentic expression of their true self.

Our partners who come into our lives have a soul contract to provide us with a mirror to help us learn and grow. Sometimes these are short windows of time, and sometimes these relationships last a lifetime. When we take the time to do our inner work, as well as the work we can harness when coming together, the most growth, healing and awakening happens.

Red Tantra is a powerful practice for bringing a couple to the most profound connection of intimacy, love, sexuality and bliss. It brings all the practices of *White Tantra*, *Pink Tantra* and *Red Tantra* into a merged practice of love, healing, sensuality and sexuality. It is the main practice that the modern US and Western Society has been drawn to. It is why people seek tantra, and initially believe they can start with *Red Tantra*. However, *Red Tantra* is an advanced art than can only be mastered, understood and truly practiced having the foundation of *White Tantra* and *Pink Tantra* under its belt. The knowledge, wisdom and experience of a true *White Tantra* Practitioner is the only person who can truly master *Red Tantra*.

In our society, many people believe they can jump into *Red Tantra* conquering and mastering their sex lives, making their sexual experiences explosive, and ecstatic with jumping straight into *Red Tantra*. However, the problem is that many people who come to practitioners and many practitioners not having proper boundaries with giving these individuals the *Red Tantra* they are seeking, often end up having serious mental breakdowns, psychological chaos, major emotional issues, and some even needing to be admitted into mental hospitals, because they attempted a practice to awaken their kundalini before they had the proper training in the gentler spiritual practice of White Tantra to prepare them for the more advanced Red Tantra.

Red Tantra can be very dangerous for those individuals who are not ready for it. It can be exciting at first, and feel orgasmic, but in the long term, the energies that have awakened only cause them to go into spasms of the energy rising through their body that can last well over a year or two or longer, and often these individuals don't know the practices to help ground them, clear them of their energies, or how to release the deep emotions in their soul that the *Red Tantra* summoned up.

In the East, *Red Tantra* is never offered or taught to anyone without at least 10 years or a lifetime of training in the art of *White Tantra*. In the west, people are impatient, impulsive, aggressive and demanding to get what they want. And so, many people have the experience of "kundalini crashes" or emotional crisis' that can cause major mental illness to come to the surface, and ultimately need medication for that mental illness to calm their system.

A True Tantra teacher and practitioner would never offer advanced practices to students who have no experience, or history of simple *White Tantra*. It is simply dangerous! Only those in the west often offer it because money is a major necessity to survive in the west, and the western culture have the money to provide to practitioners to pay their bills. And, the western peoples demand they get what they want. It is a catch 22.

Red Tantra with the long-term training of *White Tantra*, and *Pink Tantra* is a truly life altering experience. It is what the East call Tantra Sex, or Kama Sutra, and in Hinduism is the ultimate practice of connecting to the God and Goddess, or Gods and Goddesses, as they believe there are many Gods and Goddesses one can pray to and devote to. (The study of Tantra Yoga goes more in-depth into the study of mantra, which is the sacred language for praying to all the Gods and Goddesses of Ancient History).

Red Tantra is a path best known for bringing us highly connected energies of Tantra Sex. It is a practice done with your partner, primarily. It is to create a union between lover and beloved, Shiva and Shakti, and in connecting to the god and goddess of the divine, you are also connecting to the God and Goddess of each other. It is a practice of worship, and devotion and divine union. Your divine male partner becomes the Shiva, and your divine female partner, the Shakti. You each embody the God and Goddess, and when you come together to make love using ancient Tantric Sex Rituals, you join in mind, heart, body and spirit. Each of your energy centers or chakras, are aligned in union and connection with the other. There is no separation. The intention is to create peace on Earth, and bridging heaven and earth as one; transcending sex into a spiritual practice of enlightenment.

Today, there are other forms of *Red Tantra* in the West that do not require a Master to achieve any mastery. The focus of this more-worldly and material form of Tantra is largely on exploring all the pleasurable sensations you can achieve during love making. Tantric Sex is now something that couples may explore, with or without a spiritual background or practice. It is their choice, however, one must be aware of the cautions when choosing this path, as I mentioned above.

Red Tantra is known for having the ultimate ecstatic blissful experience of pleasure, joy, and orgasmic sensations. It is known as the practice of ultimate love making that can last for hours upon hours, or days on end of pleasure, leading to full body orgasm, with breaks and energies rising and falling, and reconnecting to the energies all over again during the time the couple choose to engage together while shutting out the world to be alone, and in union.

Red Tantra is a practice of building the energy and waiting for hours or days before the man releases his seed. This is the recommended practice for him to build his energy and love to the ultimate place with his Goddess. For a deep closeness to his woman, it is recommended he waits a few weeks before letting his seed go, while keeping his firmness for his woman so she can release herself over and over again. However, sometimes a woman can choose to hold hers as well, while they are building their energy together in the beginning of their energy building practice. It is up to the couple to choose how they want to build their energy together. However, the goal is that their love energies, and their spiritual energies, their heart energies, and their kundalini energies are all clear, open, cleansed, processed, and ignited and activated to the ultimate experience of themselves.

See also Tantra and Chakra Clearing, Emotional Healing and Aura Cleansing to understand the depths of how this is possible.

Black Tantra I believe is a path of combining magic and tantra in one. And magic by itself is considered very mysterious and somewhat of an unknown, except by occultists and pagan crowds. However, Black magic is considered dark magic, conjuring up revenge spells, and forcing others to do things against their will. Black Tantra when broken down in its parts has the combination of both Black Magic and ALL colors of Tantra in one. Black is the color of nothing and everything all at once. It is the color of empty space, where one can fill it with whatever they choose. So, it makes sense where Black Tantra and Dark Tantra get confused as being the same thing. However, they are not.

Black magic originally got its origins, many say, from Africa, Africans, or dark skin colored people of Egypt, and in history has been called voodoo because of these origins, and its association with curses, revenge spells, and protection magic. However, whoever came up with the term Black Tantra, their origins stemmed from combining the sacred Dakini's from ancient history, Tantra, Shamanism, and witchcraft as these Divine Goddesses were considered very powerful and God like beings, who not only had the power of Ascension, and Healing, but also the power of darkness; either removing darkness from an individual or placing it upon them to teach them lessons. They were not afraid of death, and considered death an oracle of transformation, mainly from a living human to remove something very dark within and transforming it to something very good.

However, in my experience of witnessing Black Tantra individuals, I like to call them Magicians, Masters of Magic, Masters of Energy, Masters of Sex, and Shamanism. They exude the energy of vampires, and yet, have the capacity to work with energy like Chi Gung or Tai Chi, but in an artful format of a wizard and loving black Vampire.

One is not considered dark, unless they do something of a dark nature, or harmful, or hurtful of another human being. Black Tantra can be considered dark because those individuals with that sort of power are almost Godly, and in many cases throughout history would be feared, and therefore anyone with those sort of powers in the past if discovered may be sentenced to death.

However, there are two exceptions when that sort of power is acceptable; 1. When it is requested, and 2. When one is in need of protection of another who intentionally chooses to cause another harm.

In the first situation, when Black Tantra powers are requested, the I like to call "magicians" can summon their will to pull energies out of another to release any darkness in the way of the receiver's pleasure (or those requesting the Black Tantra practitioners gifts), and channel energy up through an individual at will to cause the receivers energy to have a kundalini rising experience, and full body orgasm on the spot! They can walk into a room, spot an individual or groups of individuals, go to them and almost wave their hands, touch them in a few places, and like a magician summon their energy to pleasures of moans and bliss.

In the second situation, when one is in need of protection, it can be of an urgent matter, protecting oneself from someone mentally ill, such as narcissism or psychopathology, and in those cases, the Black Tantra, Protection magic and Vampirism are used to protect oneself from psychic harm. There are more individuals out there that try to force psychic sexual energy onto others for their manipulation than many like to admit, but using advanced practices of Black Tantra, or Black Vampirism or Protection Magic is considered acceptable in those cases, to end the attack, rather than continue to allow it to go on.

In our culture, Black Tantra has become commercialized, where people seek out those sessions because people want to have pure pleasure, ejaculation and gratification. Where as other types of Tantra, in White, Pink or Red one must utilize spiritual practices, holding in the sexual energy to build the energy to love and a more advanced place.

Black Tantrikas are often feared in India. I can see there is a lot of misconception of this path because not only is it practiced in secret, but there is also not enough knowledge or information about it. The teachings are guarded intentionally to protect it from being used in the wrong way and by those with unclear or dark intentions.

Black Tantra has not been openly practiced in the US, or really in very few places in the world. Many people have never even heard of it, and if they have very few truly understand it.

An aspect of Black Tantra that some people do know about is Sex Magic. Sex Magic has powerful intentions of energy to use ones will to manifest one's intentions. This is a practice almost identical to Magic, and specifically Grey Magic or Vampyre Magic where one uses their will and intentions to control and work with energy to create a specific goal. These practices are not done to harm another; however, the misunderstanding makes people believe the latter, and many fear and oppose the slightest of discussions.

Black Tantra is a practice that must be performed with high integrity and discretion, with full awareness, knowledge, and background in other forms of tantra. Often, it is a path that is developed after many years of practicing white, pink, and red tantra, and once the practitioner reaches a degree of awakening, certain skills and mystical powers will come naturally.

If someone wants to learn the practices of Black Tantra, they must have many years of background before they are ready to be initiated into the advanced arts of Black Tantra. Anyone interested in this path must be screened thoroughly, and pass the tests of white, pink and red tantra, and also have experienced years of spiritual practice, meditation, and their spirit and soul already in alignment with the frequencies they will advance to in Black Tantra. Often, it is a path that one will develop on their own from a lifetime of practice. It is not typically something someone can go somewhere to study or learn. I believe they must be chosen.

Here in the US, many people are skeptical and fear anything mystical or magical. If this magical Black Tantra is what you are seeking, it is possible to find it if you persist, and are willing to follow the rules of your teacher, but it tends to be a lot more difficult to find than any other types of Tantra. And, regrettably easily muddled with an entirely different form of Tantra with a name similar.

Black Tantra, as a majority or all the Tantras and as a whole, is the lesser-spoken-about branch of Tantra. After many years of advanced Tantric practice, many yogis experience siddhis or spiritual powers. These powers can be used for ceremony or personal gain. Black Tantra is an indigenous Shamanic practice, like black magic, which transforms physical energy with or without the consent of others. Throughout India today, people seek Tantrikas for hire, like witch doctors or Shamans. They are paid to end legal battles, cast spells or even burn or destroy someone's property.

Many people, without a strong foundation of spiritual practice or years of the other tantras, who begin to play with these mystical powers often get lost and lose themselves.

Instead of advancing towards spiritual enlightenment and awakening, Black Tantra can lead people in the opposite direction and away from their spiritual goals.

There is an exceptionally secret Hindu sect of Black Tantra practitioners called the Aghori. In Sanskrit, Aghori is a word that means beautiful. The Aghori's believe in getting into total darkness before they can transform into something beautiful. This is how I have lived my life and how it has shown up. The Aghori practitioners have been known to smear cremated ashes and human bones on their bodies from graveyards during ritual and celebration of life.

"Aghoris believe that every person's soul is Shiva but is covered by the *aṣṭamahāpāśa* "eight great nooses or bonds", including sensual pleasure, anger, greed, obsession, fear and hatred. The practices of the Aghoris are centered around the removal of these bonds. Sādhanā in cremation grounds destroys fear; sexual practices with certain riders and controls help release one from sexual desire; being naked destroys shame. On release from all the eight bonds the soul becomes *sadāśiva* and obtains *moksha*." (https://en.wikipedia.org/wiki/Aghori)

In other words, to go all the way into something helps one to let it go completely.

Dark Tantra is sometimes by mistake been called Black Tantra. Those that call it Black Tantra are unaware that the term Black Tantra has a completely different description and definition. This unorthodox meaning refers to a fusion of BDSM and Tantric Sex. I believe this path has surfaced more in recent times. Dark Tantra is less about the occult or mystical powers, and more about personal power, domination, bondage and submission.

My understanding is that "Dark Tantra" was "created" here in the Western culture, perhaps by people who really had a very limited or no understanding of the first meaning of Dark or Black Tantra.

Basically, Dark Tantra seems to be a sexual practice that doesn't have much to do with the basics of White Tantra, Pink or Red Tantra and their spiritual pursuits.

However, many people I have spoken to about Dark Tantra use it in a way to go deeper into their shadow self, with regards to surrendering to their partner, opening up to trust, love, acceptance, and healing parts of themselves that are hidden they wish to release through surrendering control and trusting fully in their beloved. This would be called the "Shadow Self" in psychological terms, and in my opinion why it is categorized as a form of Tantra, and not solely as BDSM.

In my journey of exploring Tantra for nearly 20 years, this is the sole reason I explore this form of tantra, and practice it to this day. It creates a level of closeness to ones beloved not experienced in other forms of tantra. It allows two people to surrender to each other to such a degree that nothing, but trust is left, and with that devoted love, commitment, and honor. It helps assist to unravel all the deepest emotional armoring, blocks, fears, insecurities, and inner child workings that most people keep dormant for fear of letting their true selves be revealed. It creates a full circle of transformation of one's self, and brings one to empowerment, expansion, and freedom of their self.

Some authors argue that there is no spiritual aspect to this Dark

Tantra. I can imagine that this could be true for some individuals who are unwilling to surrender to their beloved, do not have someone they feel safe in surrendering to, continue to keep up their guard, and create a wall of distance from others. However, this practice does help one in a committed relationship to discover the possibility of transforming this.

However, some people believe Dark Tantra is more often practiced as a form of self-expression, solely for fun, kinky play, an occasional sexual release and sexual exploration than for the purpose of spiritual awakening or enlightenment. It's up to the individuals who are practicing and their own interpretation of how they chose to see this, and also if they want to integrate both descriptions or not.

Dark Tantra or Shadow Tantra is often used to indicate an addition of BDSM or kink play. There are so many ways to play with and explore energy and jesting with power exchange in the form of submission and dominance, playing with rope, using hand cuffs, and many tools for spanking are all samples and ways to give-and-take the energy.

My Tantric Path is an eclectic one. When it comes to what I teach I would say that all of them are included. When it comes to working with new clients, I first introduce them to the path of White Tantra, with superior knowledge of energy work and breathwork, and want to make sure they are advanced enough on this path before introducing them to the next degree of Pink Tantra, and especially before moving on to more advanced practices.

When I introduce practices of Red Tantra to singles, it is mainly to teach them what to do with their partner as a guide, not as a surrogate. When they are strongly committed to a partner, or marriage, I highly suggest they come see me with their partner, rather than alone. In order to build the strongest safety net for both partners, it is best they come together, and learn and grow together along the way. When they come by themselves, they must be aware that the practices are strictly tools to use to help them build a stronger relationship with their partner, or to help remove blocks from an old relationship, or help bring in a new one. When they try to transfer their desires of intimacy or relationship onto me, they are usually terminated as a client.

The goal is to help individuals come closer together and bridge the gap of separation from the one they love the most. I, as the practitioner, am here to help transform that gap!

When a client comes alone, and chooses not to come with their partner, I am limited as to how much I can help them. The most transformation and healing happens, when both partners come together.

The best way to practice Red Tantra is with a devoted loving partner in a committed relationship.

My modalities of choice are of the heart, working with spirit and the energies of love. This practice is closest related to the heart centered practices of Pink Tantra. If you would like to speak with me about learning Tantra and creating a lifestyle for your life, through either a verbal life coaching session or a hands-on healing Tantra session, I can be reached on the links at the end of this book.

36
A Tantric Gift

As some of you know, I've been getting back into my love for crystals since I was a child. I've been collecting new crystals for my alter, my own healing and for clients. And I placed an order for a few necklaces from Singapore, with one beautiful light blue mala as a gift. And the woman who was selling these had asked me out of the blue if I would know anyone who would like a few charms from another culture with a foreign language on it, and a Temple I had never heard of. I had accepted and said if I couldn't use them, that I knew friends who could. Well, the package arrived today (after about 3 weeks since this conversation and order). I ended up opening the gift package first, and what came out of the bag blew my eyes wide open. As a Tantra Practitioner, I like surprises and can certainly handle them, and today I was a little stunned and am still laughing about it. I pulled out of the neatly packaged bag with bows and tissue paper, a set of 7 or 8 tiny little lingam charms, or in English, little tiny charms that look like penises. They are a brass or other metal with little inscriptions on the sides, and from some high energy Temple I don't know where, but I'll certainly do some research to find out. The next surprise were these large wooden size lingam's (penises) nicely packaged in a sealed plastic bag, to use for beading or other such crafting. And 2 Phra Rahu Dragon Charms.

I suppose this woman did not know the depths of my Tantric Practice, but these little gifts from the universe are a perfect metaphor and symbol that I am doing the work I am supposed to be doing, and a nice little boost to the kundalini sexual energy as well!

Rahu is the Dark Goddess in Buddhism, like Kali is to Hindu's. In Jyotish Astrology there is the Rahu and Ketu period one must overcome in each person's lifetime. Coming to the end of this period is a celebration, as this is something I myself am doing right now, but while going through it, it does take a LONG time, and honoring the darkness of life, and surrendering to those who help support it, is an act many Buddhists and Hindu's understand as a natural part of life.

Here is one similar to the metal lingham that look like the ones I have. You'll have to wait until you come visit with me again to get a closer look! It fits perfectly with my Kali, Ganesh and Tree of Life Charm necklace!

Thank you Universe!

Here are some links reflective of the beads and gifts:

http://thaiamulets-dhammapath.blogspot.com/search/label/Palakit

http://en.wikipedia.org/wiki/Wat_Bang_Phra

http://www.thaiworldview.com/bouddha/animism3.htm

37
Moon in Scorpio
Psychic Tantra

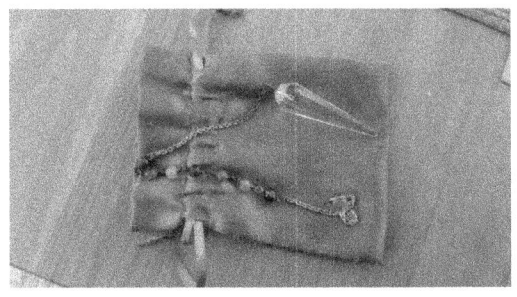

As the moon phases into full and new, each day, or two, or three days it changes the energetic vibrations on the planet. As the energies changes, so too does the astrological sign of the moon, and we move into a new vibration feeling its power and a new frequency that sometimes controls how we feel, act, think and behave. Today and yesterday we were vibrating in the energy of Scorpio, and it usually is one of my favorite moon signs the moon is phased in. The time of the moon in Scorpio, we are often in an intense place of depth for anything that we are passionate about. It is a time of mysticism, have higher prophetic visions or abilities, desire to go deeper into ourselves and discover how we feel or what it is we want. It is also a time of intense passion and sexual desires or pleasures. When the moon is in Scorpio, it is often a time of GREAT sex, and deep love making, as we are influenced and motivated to feel more passionate than normal and driven to go deeper into anything in which we love.

We also may wish to seek solitude, being alone to feel all of ourselves; loving ourselves solely in self love practices, or gentle meditation, and going deeper into our art or work and discover solutions to our work's, or life's problems via a deeper psychic ability than normal.

I am truly feeling deep gratitude at this time of my existence and ascension, and know all the profound work I have done on myself, has truly paid off, as I feel in a place of integration and balance greater than ever before. I am feeling harmonious, and utter self love and am more able to be supportive to myself and others than ever before. My psychic visions are rising, and my psychic impressions are deepening. Whatever it is that you need, I can draw from my own power and bring out the characters or energies that will support those who need me. In a sense, I can be like a Chameleon, and change to match what others need. If you put a group of people together in one room who know me, they may all have a different experience of me since I can match and draw out of myself the energies that will match and support where they are in their growth or their personal needs. My psychic channels are high during a Session, and whatever someone needs, my spirit will know, and I will sense how to support them, and in this way, I either raise my vibration and offer sexually charged Sessions, or I may tone the energies down and be softer, gentler and kinder as they may be sensitive or emotionally hurt, or I may meet them somewhere in the middle.

As the moon is in Scorpio, and moving to Sagittarius, I am moving from intense spiritual depth and Sexual energy (although this is always the case), to the more independent leadership like qualities of Sagittarius. I am truly grateful for all the love and support over these past few months and have acquired new Sea Salt lamps; that act like Air Purifiers, and new De-humidifiers to help eradicate the air issues here, and maintain a balance of pure breath and powerful health.

What's next to come are Orgone's, as in orgone therapy to raise the vibration even higher and offer another level of healing I have not given before. I also plan to acquire a set of Chakra Flat Stones to give Chakra Healing in our Tantra and Coaching Sessions, and a Chakra Pendulum to help you see with greater understanding the energies I just know need balance, and teach what I know in a more practical way. Not everyone may have my psychic gifts, and only get a hunch, and I now want to truly give you healing that will make a HUGE difference in your life for the long term.

I celebrate you as you have gifted me with YOUR presence for the many years past, and whatever years you choose to join me in the future!

Blessings and Love to ALL!

38 A Tantrikas Yoga Practice & being a Sexual Advocate Out in The World

There is a fine distinction between being the role of student and the role of teacher, however, sometimes things happen, and you can't but be your true self!

I went to an Anusara Yoga class this morning, as a student, and being the fully expressed breather that I am, I came to find that it triggered some people and "disrupted" them in the class.

I did the normal practice that everyone does. I followed the instructions on each and every pose, and very shortly after class started, my breath started to expand to its full capacity. It doesn't take long for an avid Tantrica and advocate to start moaning and groaning to practically anything that feels good in the body. I being the case, I started to breathe heavily, being so fully present and joyous to what I was experiencing I didn't notice anything going on around me.

After about an hour, when I started giggling and taking deep sighs and laid there in half straddle after a back-bend pose, the assistant teacher came over to me. She guided me to move my feet closer together to go back up in the back bend, and I really wasn't paying any attention at all to the seriousness of her or the rhythm of the rest of the class. I went out of focus and came to that euphoric place of bliss and just stayed still smiling. She looked at me again, "just move your feet closer together...a little closer." I said okay, taking a momentous breath and pushed myself back up in the back bend.

After a few minutes, I contemplated having a conversation with the teacher on asking her to "let the class know before you start that there is a Sex & Bliss Coach and Tantra Teacher visitor with us today, so if you hear extra sounds of breathing that is the reason." Instead, she told me that she had heard from quite a few people that my breathing was disrupting the others from experiencing their own breath and being in their own body. She asked me if I could, as a teacher, take the higher road and hold back my breathing to its capacity and just breathe in a normal rhythm. I felt that this would be suppressing to my own joy and I get a lot of joy out of doing a normal yoga class; perhaps much more than the average yogi.

I thought for a moment and said, "well, I could perhaps breathe out of my nose instead of out of my mouth." She said, "when you are the teacher, you can teach any way you want, but when you are wearing the students hat, I'd prefer you do your deep breathing practice at home and control your breath when you are here."

I said, "you're awesome, and I wouldn't want to not come to your class." She said, YOU'RE awesome and it was really thoughtful of you to come up to talk to me about this. And, ya know when I'm at home in my own practice, I let myself go there, but around others its different. Just think about it. It's something to meditate on."

It is something for me to think about, however, I would in no way choose to suppress my breath; especially when it comes naturally. Doing Yoga is a practice that naturally opens the breath, and if other people are not as expanded in their own bodies I cannot control that. However, what I can do is teach others how to expand themselves, so they can have the full body experience that I have. So, what I am taking out of this experience is perhaps, that yes, I am truly meant to start teaching Yoga Classes in a Tantric tone, and find avenues to do this, I have a gift to help women feel more comfortable in their bodies, I definitely need to go to another studio that is more liberal, and seeking for other alternatives of sharing myself and having a yoga practice is key. It sure is much more fun to do yoga with other people, but not if you have to change your identity in the process.

I totally love this teacher and love Anusara Yoga. So, I will try that nose breathing as a compromise next time, and if I still am disruptive, I suppose I'll seek yoga elsewhere! As a Tantrica, when you nose breathe and you are connected to your sexual kundalini energy and breath, even the nose breathing isn't so quiet! The humming and vibrational tone that comes from the throat can be just as loud, and I will consider other options.

Everything IS a choice. When it comes to choosing between feeling orgasmic or suppressed, and you *have* a choice, as a Tantrica I'll make the moans. It's much more fun, and as a Practitioner and Teacher, sometimes being self-less is the better option, AND the moaning can also be the teaching. It all depends on the audience.

I'll keep you posted!

Keep on being your true self. If you don't no one will know what you have to share with the world!

Awaken to Living; Tantra for Your Whole Life

**Section 3
Tantric Relationship**

39 Re-directing Your Marriage; Finding Your Lost Commitment

Most of us go along with our lives, doing a job, having a home, and living the mundane life of this conservative world; often forgetting what is most important to you.

Issues and triggers come up in marriage/relationships, and what many do to deal with them is find an escape; a place to go and something to distract them from what is really upsetting them in their hearts. Many think that it is not possible to get to the bottom of their relationship struggles, and in a majority of cases, the partner, significant other, husband and even the wife, will look for an escape route to their biggest pains. There are few brave souls who are willing to do the deeper work, but more often than not, couples feel distant, frustrated, hurt and alone.

How do you find your love again that is hidden inside your heart? You find it by taking responsibility for your actions, your behaviors, your ways of being and being authentically honest with what you are truly feeling; the pain that has turned into resentment, the anger that has turned into rage, and the sadness that has turned into despair. When you can come to the truth of who you are, speak this truth and communicate it verbally or through written letter, a new peace can replace the darkness that you are carrying around with you.

Many come to me looking for an escape, and yes, I can certainly offer you an escape, however, the goal is not to maintain an escape and continue looking for ways of running away, but instead running towards that which you are most fearful of; your own feelings, your own emotions and your hidden self inside your heart. When you can find the truth within you, and be truly authentic about how you've been behaving towards yourself and towards the ones you really love, your true love for your loved ones will return to you, and in your love returning to you, you get to be a different way with those in your lives. And in your being a person who authentically shows love, forgiveness, acceptance and peace towards those you care about the most, they then will give you in return, what you have deeply longed for all along.

My wish for you, is that you learn to be authentic to your own behaviors, take responsibility and allow a new vulnerability with yourself and your loved ones to awaken, and in this awakening, you get everything you ever dreamed of.

40 Energetic Alignment in Relationships

Opening your heart is not an easy task, but when one is ready and has the desire, you can only continue this task. It is not about making someone else wrong, or fixing the other person, but instead, seeing the other person as your own mirror and reflection of the pain within your own body; as the interaction with them brings this out in you. As you heal, they heal. And as such, as they heal, you heal as well. Blaming the other, or putting demands on the other to meet your needs is never how you will go about getting your needs met. When you can fill those needs in yourself, or with others and allow things to come to you rather than blaming the person in front of you, or pushing those needs on them, everything else will fall into place, as you desire and eventually as you need them. But the need that most know of in this culture, is an unhealthy need based on attachment and fear. A need based on love and a giving through unconditional love is the only real kind of love to live for.

I know through experience what it feels like for someone to take their love away from you. The pain of breaking an interaction or a wall being built from someone you loved so deeply and connected with so deeply, and choosing to walk away just as quickly, is one of the most painful challenges we will all face as humans. But a human also who is here to evolve, grow and transform their mind and body into a human of pure light, knows that the dark needs from insecurity and fear will only wear you down and deplete your energy, from a feeling of lack, of looking outside, instead of within. Looking for your needs to be filled outside yourself will only continue the quest of looking for those needs to be filled outside yourself.

It is time now to take your power back, and own the lack of integrity you are placing on others as your own responsibility. You are the only person who can give you all of your energy, and anywhere it is lacking is only a lack in your own soul.

Take all the space you need. Separate from others and run or walk away from this pain, but it can also be interpreted as an avoidance to your own pain. All the other wants to do is love you, but your neglect in facing the issue that is deeply wanting to be released from yourself, will only force you to face the pattern within yourself again later. Perhaps now you are not ready to look at yourself, but sooner or later you might have to.

Hoping and wishing for an answer, is never the solution. Doing the work, the hard work, is the only solution to completion, to internal transformation, an inner knowing and love. Your loved ones are just being themselves, but your response, reaction and interaction is where you hold the power. When you can allow others to be who they are, and love them just the same, love will always remain. When there is blame, need or expectation from someone that is outside yourself, you are only setting yourself up for failure. The only result is upset. Often times the upset from others is the mirror to your own upset inside yourself. When you can truly love yourself and be with all of who you are, loving others becomes simple. The task can be removed and all that is left is bliss, love and joy.

Many people look for the easy way out, but the easy way out only brings more of the same things you will have to go through again and time again. The rewards of doing the work are worth the effort, and you only have you to be proud of in the end. No one else gets the benefits. No one else gets the reward; only you.

The imbalance in relationships starts in the self. And since the imbalance starts in you, it is only you who can change it. Love just is. Anything that doesn't look like love is only fear trying to heal.

41
Communication To Create The Intimacy You Really Want!!!

Many people don't realize how powerful communication affects your intimate life. Many take their relationships for granted and expect them to always be the same, doing what they have always been doing. Many don't understand the significance that your words create your reality. Every single word that comes out of your mouth, or that stays quiet, has an impact on the people in your life and the reality you live in. People expect to go walking around life doing what they have always been doing, and expecting to get different results.

All that is necessary in creating the love life of your dreams, is instead of making yourself and your needs a priority, is in making your partner know that they truly matter.

It takes authenticity, integrity, honesty, and being real with your partner, where in the past you have been lying, keeping secrets, putting you first, blaming and making wrong, having expectations, withholding, criticizing, and being defensive. In other words, taking responsibility where you have been irresponsible is all that is necessary in cleaning up your communication and creating the intimacy you truly long for.

If you have been coming home late from work everyday, putting your personal life first, your needs first all the time, not listening to what is important to your partner, and getting mad and defensive at them for being upset about it, you can't expect them to feel loved by you and want to be intimate with you later after all is done and the end of the night is near. Can you? Think about it. You are in a one-person relationship when you are doing this, and then expecting your partner to want to have sex with you at the end of the day. It's actually ridiculous if you think about it. All people need validation for how they feel, they want to know that their feelings matter, they want to feel accepted, loved and supported in every way and they want to be made important by you, a priority. However, if sex or any of your other needs is all that matters to you, what your left with is a one hand show.

Learning how to touch your partner, having the most wonderful tantra techniques to give her (or him) the pleasure they want is only beneficial when you have the closeness in their heart, and they are truly open to being with you this way. It is easy to have great sex and beautiful intimacy in the beginning of your relationship, but try taking on being responsible for your actions and your words, and you might just fall in love again. Tantra practices are nothing without the closeness, respect, safety and honesty of your heart. Your relationship is only half of what it can be without true integrity!

42 Voicing Your Truth

Do you often have trouble telling your partner how you really feel? Do you find it frustrating knowing that you are keeping things hidden from the one you love? Would you rather create the depth of intimacy that true honesty creates in a relationship?

I often find that my lovers have a difficult time hearing the truth. Either they are not ready to hear what I have to share, or they are completely numb to their feelings in the first place that anything that makes them feel is too strong of an outside force almost prompting them to go inside to their hidden cave, where they would rather not know anything at all.

More often than not, it is men who have a hard time with feelings. Women on the other hand are Master of It. Men are like the rock, the intellectual experts, the scientists, the thinkers who have strong opinions about what they think and are compelled to find solutions through their thoughts. Women on the other hand are like the flower, they are the softness, the feminine water running down stream. They are adaptable and can change form to fit their surroundings. Women are the mothers, the lovers, the compassionate innocence and hold the key for love that we are desire. Finding a balance between the masculine and feminine energies within ourselves is what we need and what will ultimately allow us to be the voice to our hearts.

It is like the innocent child who screams when he gets mad, or cries when his feelings are hurt. Children are our greatest teachers in getting to our deepest feelings. As adults, we've become numb to the temptations of allowing ourselves to surrender to that foreign territory, that as children it was second nature. So, my recommendation is to scream when you are mad, cry when you are sad, and take rest always when you need it. Don't ever hold anything inside.

Learn from your children, and let them teach you how to feel. There is no depth in our closest relationships without it.

43 Intimacy to Healing

It is a beautiful experience when one can allow themselves the pleasure of pure and innocent connection, love, holding and cuddling! Sometimes new energy opens, expands, clears and heals in this innocent encounter. Cuddling with a stranger is a beautiful thing, but cuddling with someone you love, feel deeply safe with, connected and care for is a whole different experience. Perhaps your Beloved, your husband or wife in sharing this cuddling is an ultimate high, to allow your heart to flow back to its true fluidity, and open up to intimacy, sensuality and sexuality. In this, sex can become a gentle, tantric, healing experience!

I love when my heart opens after deep energetic cuddling and connection! I love when my energy lifts, clears, and is filled with divine sacred union. I am grateful for the awareness of this energy, and the love within my heart!

Who have you cuddled with lately?

What have you gotten out of its experience?

Have you cuddled with a friend, a lover, a boyfriend/girlfriend, husband or wife?

How did this make you feel?

Did it open you up to deeper intimacy with someone else, your significant other, husband/wife?

Did it warm your heart and make you feel more connected to the universe/appreciation?

I'd love to hear what it created for you, and how it inspired you! Please use this blog as a means to write for yourself!

44 Letting Your Heart Open

After it has been months, or even perhaps years, after a relationship has ended (even if it was over before it was officially over), its a risk to open your heart again. Its important to take the time after the ending of a relationship to mend your heart, grieve, and let go of the past. However, when a new person, who you fancy, desire, have attraction for, and matches who you are, your vibration, your life practices, the things you love, your compatibility, perhaps your spirituality, and you have similar goals and desires for life, it seems like a fit. When your chakras are aligned or the level of awakening and development you have accomplished is a match to someone, it feels like you're in heaven. Why not take the risk, and surrender to someone like this?

Well, after not having been with someone in a while, it can be scary. It takes guts to your open heart again. It takes being brave, especially to those who have gone through such challenging relationships in the past. But once you have loved, the ability to love will always return. Sometimes you need a little push. And, someone who's a match is a perfect push to jump over that edge.

Have you ended a relationship not too long ago, and have fear of diving in with someone new? Are you afraid to get too close? And, if you feel like you're getting close, do you immediately start to pull away or push away as soon as it gets comfortable?

Letting your heart open is a brave and amazing thing. It feels magical, like bliss, heaven, and the feeling of a new love, a new sweetheart can be scary, but it also can be utterly exciting! You don't know the other person that well yet. You are in the discovery, the exploration, the journey, the ride. Let it be fun! Take the risk, and ride the wave of love! You might just land in the other persons arms, and be embraced with love like you've never known.

And, you do never know. The unknowing can be scary, and it can also be fun!

45 When You Want Your Husband and Someone else shows up!

When You Want Your Husband and Someone Else Shows Up. This is the pitfall of many relationships. A woman is craving connection with the man she loves, and what happens is that her man is unavailable. He's busy or preoccupied, or his interest has dwindled, and he has other concerns and things he wants to focus on. She's deeply saddened and desperate to gain his attention, but he's always somewhere else, emotionally or physically.

In a Polyamorous Marriage this is perfectly fine. There is an agreement between both partners that they are allowed to be with other lovers, so long as the structure of the relationship is maintained. However, if the foundation of the marriage is rocky, or there has been very little connection, intimacy and commitment between the two partners, straying from the marriage can feel like cheating, or in Christian terms "committing adultery".

When you're in love with your husband (or significant beloved) and there is no intimacy, your heart tears up inside. You want his commitment. You want his willingness to do what it takes to be there for you, stay by your side and give you his all! But when you have waited and waited for him to show up in this way, and all of a sudden someone else shows up, most of the time, it is like God giving you the gift you have been waiting for! You fall prey to this new amazing being that you are so deeply drawn to, and your wish has been granted. Then the big question is: what do you do next? Do you continue to wait for the man you deeply love, or do you continue to fall into the arms of another? How long are you truly willing to wait? If waiting is putting your life on hold, perhaps waiting is not what your supposed to be doing anyway. Perhaps, you ARE supposed to be enjoying life and just surrender to what life gives you!

46 Intimate Love with Your Partner

Most people dream about being close to the person they love the most. They often wake up from dreams in the morning of their wife or husband that they are distant or separated from; just succumbing to the what's so. Their heart aches to be close to them; even though their mind often tells them they don't like this about them, or that, or that they'll never agree or be able to compromise on anything. Couples often stay in the wishful thinking stage, or suppressing their truest hearts desires and just accepting that the relationship won't get any better, when in fact, this is simply not true.

Perhaps you are blaming yourself for your relationship being distant, or you are blaming your partner, and put all your anger on him or her. Perhaps you've given up on the relationship all together because you don't know what's possible, and you end up believing what you truly desire is not possible at all.

Many women stay in an unhappy relationship, not knowing how to change things, or their partner and wishing he will change. Many men don't make an effort at all; even though they tell themselves they want to heal the relationship or be close to their wife, and go to a mistress, a sex parlor, an erotic salon, a sex surrogate, or an escort just to try to fill the void and lack of intimacy they are getting with the partner they really love. They make no effort to heal the root cause; nor try to heal their own issues so that his wife might fall back in love with him all over again.

But what men and women both crave deeper than anything in the world, is to feel a deep intimate connection with the person they love, that they married or are in a committed relationship with. People don't want to have to go to other lovers, or temporary affairs to avoid the pain of the distance with their partner. What their heart craves more than anything, is to be held and caressed in the arms of their lover, their wife or husband and to know that the person they deeply love, cares for them, accepts them, and deeply desires them and loves them in return. It is a dream come true when their beloved can return their love to the man or woman they are the closest to, and fall in love all over again with the same person.

It is totally possible that you can fall in love again, with the same person, and in fact, fall in love with this same person over and over again! I can help you fall in love again, and remove the emotional pain, blocks, upsets and disappointments that have gotten in the way of the innocent freshness and intimate love you deserve!

47 A Thriving Relationship

The difference between a thriving relationship and sinking a rocky boat~

Being pro-active ~
Turning your relationship to amazing:

Impeccability
Being Responsible - & Being Willing to be Wrong
Trust
Integrity
Honesty
Vulnerability
Acknowledgment
Honoring Your Word
Surrender
Kindness
Consideration - Putting the Others Needs First
Respect
Selflessness - Giving without Receiving - Loving
Being Present
Listening
Patience
Flexibility
Speaking the Truth & Communicating
Being a Team, supporting each other even you you're not around, your dreams, visions, goals and desires

**Being lazy ~
Turning your relationship to sour:**

Judgment
Expectations
Placing Blame
Holding Grudges
Trauma or Being Incomplete with your past
Anger or Resentment
Comparing
Lack of Acknowledgment
Taking for Granted/Assuming they will always be there
Not Appreciating
Being Lazy, Procrastinating or not Following Through on what you said
Needing to Be Right
Lack of Commitment - Doing Everything but spending time together
Selfishness - Only Considering how you feel, expecting to get what you want, getting your needs met and not the others
Attachment
Jealousy/Possessiveness
Manipulation
Keeping Secrets & Lack of Communication
Doing what you want, despite what the other person feels. ~ A Solo Team

It's much easier to be lazy than to be pro-active, but if you want to keep your relationship, revitalize your intimacy and be filled with love, there are some things to consider.

48 To Be Loved By A Man

I know what it feels like to be loved by a man; a man whose heart is open wide to the spirit you are; a man who loves you, or in the moment feels as though he is deeply in love with you.

To be held in his arms; to feel his breath upon your chest, as he holds you in embrace, and caresses your heart into deep utter relaxation.

To be teased into bliss by the simplicity of his eyes melting into yours.

You never forget what it feels like to be held by a man; a man, not a boy, or a child, and not your father or your son. A man, who is so deeply in love with YOU!

His rich smell as his pheromones reach out to yours and tantalize your adrenaline into heaven.

A spark of simplicity, a whimper in your heart of relief, of satisfaction, of knowing you are woman, as you are received in his love, and accepted for being the Goddess you are!
What a gift you are receiving, in being loved by his depth, in knowing you ARE Goddess, and are powerful in your femininity; a divine being worthy of being loved.

What a gift he is receiving, in giving him the experience of loving you, in knowing he is capable of loving and valuable in being received.

To be loved by a man offers so many gifts; for the receiver and the giver. To be a woman, being loved by a man helps you to know you ARE alive, and you are worthy, are capable and acceptable in being a Woman; a wise woman, an innocent woman, a powerful woman, a vulnerable woman; that you are allowed to be YOU, and you are allowed to be Goddess. You have permission and you need not shut down your prowess, your sensuality or your love!

Some thoughts to consider:

1). What does it mean to be loved by a man to you?

2). As a man, what does it offer you to love a woman? And, what does it mean to you to love a woman, who truly receives your love?

3). As a woman, what gifts do you receive when you open your heart to receiving the love from your beloved man that is right there in front of you?

4). As a woman, how often do you allow yourself to be loved by your husband/boyfriend?

5). Are there times when you shut him out and choose not to be embraced by him? If Yes, what causes you to close down to the one you love the most? (What thoughts are going through your mind? Are you resigned, cynical, blaming, judgmental, or resentful? Do you feel unloved? Do you feel unaccepted? Do you feel threatened and not supported? Do you lack trust? Do you feel guilty or wrong? Do you feel betrayed? Are you angry? Do you want to forgive? Are you stressed and feel powerless? Are you afraid and want to feel safe?)

6). Are you a woman, married or partnered to a man, going through your own emotional crisis and don't feel understood or accepted for who you are? Do you wish to be understood? If you felt safe and accepted, how would you go about explaining to your man what you are dealing with, so he could be a team player to help you get through your current struggles?

7). Do you feel as though, you are accepted, but still can't talk to him about your inner world? Are you afraid of being judged or that he will stop loving you? What's the worst thing that could happen if you told him what you felt?

8). Are you a woman (or a man) who doesn't like talking about feelings and wishes the problems or issues would just go away? Would you rather wish them away then deal with them? What are you afraid of that makes you want to run when it comes to feelings?

9). If you had it your way, how would you want your current relationship to look like, feel like and smell like? (What would your surroundings and environment be, how would your partner behave towards you, how would they treat you, how would you treat them, where would you live, and what would you have in your home, how would you get along with in-laws and friends in social outings? etc.)

10). Are you the typical leader in your relationship and the first to bend to work out an argument, or are you the one who holds grudges and waits to see if, maybe, things will work out on their own? If you did become the leader, what would you do or say to your partner to help them open their heart to you again?

Bonus Question:

11). If you are not receiving the type of love that you really want, ask yourself, what is it that you want, and what in your relationship is missing, if you had it your way, you would want to be there?

If you're a man reading this, you are welcome to copy this and print it out to give to your beloved woman. (You are also welcome to turn the questions around to address yourself as a man). If you are a woman, consider reading this and answering the questions for yourself. You may discover some things about yourself, your relationship, hidden desires, and you may get to experience what it is that is really important to YOU!

49 Withholding Your Love

When you withhold love from the people you love, what is it you are gaining? Are you withholding in order to protect yourself? Are you holding onto resentment or regret? How long will you continue to hold onto these feelings? Are you doing it because you feel you are right? How does it feel to be right? Does it make you feel strong, proud, confident or some other emotion?

Choosing to be right is the old paradigm of communication and only creates distance, separation, upset, and keeps your-self under control; rather than dealing with how you really feel; a loss for the connection to the person you love.

How many people do you choose to withhold your love from? If you think about it, there are probably at least half a dozen people you are withholding love from. If you are not feeling utter peace and joy in the presence of those you care about, you are withholding love; even in the subtlest capacity.

Withholding your love keeps your body in an armored state; your chest becomes tighter, your breathing is more shallow, your body feels rigid and anxious.

When you're upset at the person you love the most and holding on to anger in your body while taking your time to get over the anger, having a hard time releasing the anger, or hoping eventually it will go away, no matter what you will be withholding your love from this person, AND withholding love from yourself as well. When you are not present to your anger or upset, it may feel like it is the other person's fault. But in fact, you are the only person who can forgive and let this go.

What do you do when you are upset at the person you love? Do you take hours, weeks, months, or years to forgive? When you have upset or anger, do you decide to date someone else? Hang out with your friends instead.

50 Your Partners Needs vs Yours

When we make our partners needs, and in particular their sexual needs, more important than our own, we lose ourselves in the pursuit in making them happy. We may think we are helping them and doing them a favor, however, they were not originally attracted to us because we gave up our power, passion, and drive for them. In essence, we lose our control, our life force and our value for living when we give in always to someone else's needs.

When we let go of control, and surrender to someone else's it does something to our spirit, our heart, our relationship with the other person, but also the relationship to ourselves and all the other relationships in our lives. We get lost in the mess of the relationship and become something; someone else. It's like the expression "trying to fit a square peg into a round hole" and it never works!

It is important to honor someone else's feelings, beliefs, opinions and needs, however, not at the expense of your own, and in particular not at the expense of one's own life. Sometimes we can forget who we are, and forget ourselves during that drive to make someone else happy. However, if the other person, your partner, does not honor, value and hold your own feelings, needs, beliefs and opinions up high and shuns them, ignores them and just quietly smiles that he (or she) is getting everything they need and want and avoiding you, the relationship is not worth staying in. In psychological terms, one might call that a Narcissistic Abusive Relationship, but on more common terms, the relationship is just not healthy, and definitely not balanced.

There MUST be balance for a relationship to work. There must be a healthy give and take, and if someone is getting something at the expense of the other person and incapable of seeing how they are hurting the other person, only doing their best to manipulate, coerce and control them, it is definitely a toxic relationship.

Sometimes people have to throw themselves into the fire over and over again until they finally learn their lesson, and finally learn that what they are doing to themselves might be harming them. I threw myself into the fire, and did it again and again, until I truly got the lesson. "My life is NOT about someone else; it is about myself, and no one can save you but yourself! My life is about living NOW; not next year; not next month and NOT in ten years. It is about today; for today is all we have!" And when we give up our passion to make someone else happy, and in particular to make sure they do not become unhappy or angry, it is definitely considered abusive! I am on clear alert that after all the power surged through me to stand up for myself, I am moving to the place of standing up for others as well. I claim the position to be a stand for all women and children to be protected and loved, and that men truly get the help they need when they need it, and for all to open their hearts to surrender to their truth and look inside for the answers!

> Make your life your own, and on occasion hold someone else's hand, (but not at the expense of yours)!

51 The Dominant Woman

Hey guys, are you tired of being bossed around and controlled by your wife (or girlfriend)? Do you have to live a secret life in order to maintain some sense of control and sanity? Do you feel scared she's going to catch you in the act, for making secret phone calls to someone you like or have an interest in? Do you have to maintain a level of privacy and secrecy in order to keep your head on straight and make sure your head will not be CHOPPED off when you walk home or come back into her arms? What would happen if you did get caught? Would she go to the drastic measures of divorce or a break up, just because you wanted to live a normal healthy life, and express yourself with someone who wants to listen?

This is the trap many relationships live in today. One feels unheard, misunderstood; the other wants to maintain control, power and dominance and the two have to keep secrets, lies and shut out the truth from the other. Jealousy is born, possessiveness and control and a war for authority and dominance. What usually happens to relationships that are living in this reality, this lie, and have to pretend they are something they are not? Often, over time, they separate, they divorce or break up, and many times shutting out the other completely from their lives with little room for resolution or healing.

Probably if the truth came out today, the worse that could happen would be separation; the best, a best friend again, someone you could feel close to, safe with, and a deeper love than before healing. What would happen if the truth came out? Or, even better, if the couple were honest with their needs, wants and desires before any problems arose?

When a woman shows up with her fierce rage about her man "jeopardizing" their relationship for his own self-worth and personal fulfillment, a man shuts down. He pulls back and creates more separation. The woman feels she has a sense of control and is keeping her man on her leash, so he will not run away from her, and "they maintain their commitment". However, do they really maintain their commitment, or is it under false pretenses? lies, secrets and dominance.

Men DO NOT want to be dominated, just as much as women don't. However, when a woman tries dominating her man, she is only pushing him away further and getting less and less over time the thing she actually wants; her man.

When women can let go of their jealously and control, and men can speak their truth, the world will be a happier place. All the secrets create a sort of conspiracy and controlled, repressed, and conservative relationship. The relationship is not free, it doesn't feel open, it doesn't feel good, and it gets harder and harder to stay! In order for a relationship to thrive, be your true self to your Beloved, and then you get to be your true self to you! It doesn't get any better!

52 Sexual Flirtations with Your Beloved

I like to play games with love, and call upon my power to assert what it is that I desire. I don't question it, it just arrives, and I follow as my heart calls.

When you become the warrior to your lover, you can open his/her heart and whatever was there before that moment has a chance to be released, be free and be gone! It is such a joy to seduce your partner into the pleasures of the moment, even if those moments are just a tease and the time is limited to truly be alone, that one tease can create an opening of something so much more!

What is it that you are doing to seduce your partner? How does your partner like to be seduced? Perhaps all you have to do is be yourself!

53 When You're in the Mood and Your Hunny Isn't

A story and some Coaching:

Upon waking in the morning, I was horny as a banshee. I looked over at my hunny and he was simply out cold! I was up and ready to go. Our son was sleeping in the bed beside us. Since we have a toddler, we often sneak out of the bedroom before he wakes and slip into another room to have a rendezvous in the morning, or a late hour snack. I tried comforting him to waking, but he still would not move. I cuddled him, caressed him, moved my body into his, leaned into his shoulder and put my face on his shoulder, breathing and making deep sounds... letting him know in my own way I was fully alert, awake and ready for some love making! My hips were rocking, I was breathing heavy and I tried taking his hand to lift him and walk him into the other room, but he did not budge.

What do you do when you're excited to connect to your loved one and they are either not interested, not horny or are just completely exhausted?

In the past I would massage him and caress him for about a half an hour to wake him up and eventually he would, but this time, we were running out of time and doing all my tactics of convincing and seducing for a half an hour was not an option. And then, I went to set up the other space and when I came back he was cuddled up nicely next to our son and solid as a rock in this next place. Within a few minutes our son woke up, and that opportunity was lost.

I started grunting, and still wanted to escape to the other room; letting our son be alone for 5 to 10 minutes. It didn't happen.

So, instead I decide to shift all that creative energy to getting ready in the morning, getting my son's school box ready and to make myself available for clients later. Thanksgiving is this week and we agreed we would sleep together Thanksgiving night and I would sacrifice a portion of my Friday morning to be with him, with the intention to sneak again somewhere we could be alone for a few minutes. Our schedules are conflicted with time to be alone, and with his new job, my role as a mother, and our son either being in school or with one of us, being alone isn't always easy. So, I take advantage of those few opportunity's we do have, and trust that eventually we will take another date night alone, and make some time for a couple hours of a rendezvous for ourselves!

The best way to deal with these kinds of situations is to 1). Come from a place of non-attachment, 2) do not judge, 3). Speak words of kindness, 4). Accept your partners needs, wants and their concerns as well, 5). Make a new promise or agreement for the future, and 6). Take care of yourself today in the best way for you!

54
Heart Opening

I am so utterly and deeply grateful for this past week's experience, of heart opening, divine inner union, peace and love, and deep connected healing intimacy. As a practitioner, I too, need nurturing, love and connectedness from those who are not my followers or clients, but also to those on a personal intimate level. It has been near one year since my Beloved and I parted ways, and I knew this time, it would sadly be the last. I've taken this past year in grieving, letting go, and doing what I could to heal my heart. However, the experience this past week took me over the edge of that heart opening in a way that has been needed for perhaps years.

I went to a spiritual retreat, one that had similarities near and dear to my heart. I've been going to see Amma since 1999, however, this event, was unique. Not only did I get to experience the love, kindness and healing of the guru who was leading the retreat, but also got to experience a connected love with a special being who was at this retreat.

Perhaps we were breaking a rule, in connecting on an intimate level, however, my heart was screaming yes, and my spirit was leading the way. My soul made the choice to follow this feeling, and in doing so, my heart got to receive a deep connection of love that had kept it guarded for many years. A being who shares love, without concern, without judgment, or body armor, and can just be in the moment, listening, with presence, being intuitively guided, and following his own heart, speaks loudly to my own being. To be touched with divine presence, listening, and an inner knowing, left me speechless, and in absolute joy. My heart broke open as tears ran down my face. He had no idea how long I had been waiting for this heart connection, one that I cannot teach. This way of being must come from within. This way of being must already be known from the lover connecting to the lover. I cannot make another person learn how to be present, to know how to love without pressure, or neediness, clinginess, demanding energy or fear. Whoever, you are, you must come from a place of deep love, and this love is already a part of you. I am grateful to have connected with a being who could offer this, and offer it without expectation.

When a woman receives love in such a way, she has an opportunity to open up her flower, to open up her beauty, her radiance, her power, her pleasure and her joy. She cannot be forced to connect with another. She cannot be expected to be wide open immediately. She must trust her inner knowing, her instincts, and her truth. In this, an expansiveness arises and healing returns!

> He inspired me to let go of worry, and write a book about a topic most definitely needed. I am jumping on this creative passion right now!

55 Tantra and Intimacy

You're in bed with your hunny, and she's laying on her side, facing the other direction. You're horny as a firecracker and you can't seem to get anything to make her turn over and make love to you. You wish you could get some satisfaction and pleasure her and feel fulfilled yourself.

You had an argument earlier that day. In fact, you have many arguments many days and they seem to go on and on. Now that you think about it, this has been going on for months, maybe even years. But you're still that horny little fire cracker you were when you first met. Your Sexual drive is as high as its ever been, but the love between the two of you is missing. You wish you could just make love and have it all go away, but that never seems to work. And, now you're laying in bed, its late at night and you have the perfect opportunity to make love, and she isn't into it. (or you aren't).

When it comes to Tantra, anything will turn you on, but when it comes to intimacy, someone's heart is broken, and you don't know why or how to mend it.

Healing the heart of the person who is withdrawing, withholding and suppressing is not an easy task. That person must be willing to heal it, address, it, look at the core of what is driving his or her behaviors, and learn to forgive, oneself and the other.

If it is not you, and you love your partner, try making suggestions that he or she work on healing this with you, or alone. If he or she is not willing to look at his or her own self, and you still want to stay with this partner, now it is your journey to do your own work. You may discover hidden feelings why you stay, or chose to accept your partner as they are. Or perhaps, you may realize, it is time to move on.

The only way to connect to your beloved is if both partners are willing to look at themselves. It is not a one-person relationship, and it is not a one-person journey of healing either.

56 Pulling Passion Out of a Hat

Where does passion come from? What do you do with it when it overwhelms you? But more importantly, how to you access it when it is in hiding?

When passion disappears, what do you focus on? How do you regain the joy and pleasure in your relationships if no passion exists between you and your Beloved?

Sometimes, and most often, passion sizzles after it has peaked to its high with an affair, and especially with those people we love oh so much and see sometimes more often than our spirits perhaps want to. It is our hearts that want them around, but in the hanging around, the energy sizzles, the spark, as they say, runs out, and the drive to be together can disappear overnight!

When you're in love with your husband or wife, and you wish to remain in love with them, it is almost crucial to make a date night (or day) with them to keep the sizzle high! That sizzle is what drives us, it moves us and excites our juices to be with them, and to be with them again and again! We can forget the importance of someone in our lives when you see them often, and you can definitely forget what it feels like to be touched, caressed and fondled by their flesh!

Every single part of our bodies have desire in them and the ability for passion and pleasure. The simplest touch on a face, or pressure on an arm can arouse desires forgotten and misplaced for mundane habits in the home or workplace. When you want to turn that heat on, try teasing your lover! Remind them of your sensual power. Remind them that you truly can turn them on! AND, remind yourself you can turn yourself on too! Sometimes, in order to turn on someone else, you must turn on yourself first! And sometimes to turn on yourself, you must remember who you are, and what matters to you, and that your luscious body deserves to be touched, pampered and caressed with love! Your lover is waiting for you and your heart is always ready to be filled; even if you forget that it is there! It surely is!

57 Intimacy and Touch

In this short Intimacy and Touch segment, you be will lead through a few simple intimacy practices great for couples to do together to increase their bond, trust, safety and intimacy with one another. This practice can also be done with a stranger to help with opening your heart, learning to accept people for who they are, to see their greatness, and building the ability to let down your guard, gaining love for yourself, the ability to receive love, but also give. It helps to create a balance of giving and receiving in yourself, and find the beauty and love in everything you see. The practice helps increase your appreciation for your loved one, but also life in general. To appreciate life, is to feel grateful, and with gratitude all your desires can be manifest. The practice also helps one to be seen, witnessed, and often when we are witnessed in our true authentic nature, we can more easily be our true self with others, those we love, but also strangers and life itself. To be authentic is to be the real you, and nothing creates joy more than by being who you are.

In this practice of Intimacy and Touch, couples will have an opportunity to get closer and learn a couple simple practices you can take home with you. You can also partner with someone new, and learn how to be vulnerable with a new person and feel safe knowing, it is new for them too.

Some practices during the 15-minute segment will be:
Belly Breathing while Eye Gazing, 5 minutes or longer as time permits for eye gazing, starting with the belly breath to get grounded and connected with your partner.
Scanning their body with your hands, non-Touch, find out where your partner felt the energy and where they did not
Firm holding pressure as your partner allows, slowly going into the position and slowly coming out.

58 Celebrating Spiritual Relationship

Today I want to talk about Spiritual Relationship and what that means. I'm sure many of you have an understanding on some level of what spiritual relationship means to you, and perhaps you already have a beautiful relationship where you surrender to the others feelings and moments as they show up, but there are fewer people who are in long term relationships and in love than there are those who feel separate, distant and alone.

When you were in love, and a relationship was new, do you remember how you used to put your beloved's feelings first, and you really listened and made sure you did what you knew would make them happy? Perhaps you practiced a little more self love and perhaps even, gave a little more of yourself, were more patient and understanding and accepted your new lovers pros and cons a little better. Perhaps all the upsets and triggers didn't exist to you then, and you were just in the state of bliss and the euphoria of "new love"!

Well, what happens after this new glow is gone? What do you do to regain the feeling of love, and bring back the state of bliss and joy when your heart sang in the beginning of a new relationship? Do you still give your lover gifts for no reason? Do you still dress in the way you know he or she would absolutely adore? Do you still wear clothes that you know would turn him or her on? Do you still surprise your lover just because you want to see him/her? Do you send your love notes or gifts in the mail that would drop their jaw? Do you make date nights/days where NO ONE can disturb you, and you have time to be alone to do what makes the BOTH of you happy?

When a relationship is old, perhaps distant or sour, try re-creating a new meaning for the relationship and change the way you see it; change the boundaries and let go of what you were holding on to.

Change the expectations and surrender your heart to your Beloved. Notice your anger, your disappointment or your sadness, and do YOUR inner work to change yourself; rather than trying to change the situation, or worse, the other person.

Do you have a spiritual practice you can do to help you in your heart, to clear your energetic space, or your inner world? Try on a new meditation practice, a simple breathing meditation or a simple mantra practice; something you can do on a DAILY basis that will help you to come back to your heart EVERY time you notice your heart is getting hard or filling with anything other than love! You might notice your life change and you might just fall in love with your Beloved all over again!

59 When To Go Past Dating

How do you know when to take your relationship past the dating point? How do you know when to start kissing, being intimate, or becoming sexual? If you want the relationship to last, and not be just a sexual fling, it is often best to avoid deeper acts of sex and intimacy until you know for sure the relationship feels solid. There is that rocky stage in a new relationship where you want to be intimate, but you also want it to be the real thing. How do you know how long to wait and when to go past dating? Do you wait one month, three months, or four? Timing can be everything for each couple, and each individual.

It is crucial to discover how serious the person you are dating is, especially if you want something serious. And if you find out two months in, they don't want anything serious, its much easier to walk away if you haven't had sex. But what if you have? Then what do you do? Do you walk away as soon as you know your goals are different? Or do you wait it out to see if perhaps the other person is not sure yet?

Most of the time, if someone tells you in the beginning of a relationship, that they don't want anything serious, you should really listen to them. If they tell you they just want to have fun, or want to remain celibate, or are not looking for long-term commitment, you should take whatever words they say literally. Their actions may be different than their words, but it's the words in the very beginning that define how they will truly be later. If someone hints to you that they "think" maybe they are Bipolar, or that they have had a history of being afraid after things start to get serious, and hide or pull away, LISTEN to them! All of these initial honest clues will impact the rest of your relationship, and if they told you these things from the beginning, you WERE forewarned!!!

If your date, warned you about some major things that would impact your dreams of a healthy and serious relationship, and you didn't listen, that's your fault! You need to be the one to walk away, and you need to be the stronger one; not them. They are wounded, scared, conflicted, confused, or perhaps just a jerk. You need to be the wise one! And choose whether to go past dating and of deeper into the relationship, or end it!

It is best NOT to have any sexual intimacy with someone until you know for sure who they are, their habits, beliefs, goals, if you could be good friends, if they are healthy, if you are compatible, and if you can really see yourself with them for the long term. When you jump in right away, not truly discovering their true colors, things get sticky and challenging, and it only causes more pain later. Be smart, and wait. Trust your gut, and listen to your heart!

60 Letting Your Heart Open

After it has been months, or even perhaps years, after a relationship has ended (even if it was over before it was officially over), its a risk to open your heart again. Its important to take the time after the ending of a relationship to mend your heart, grieve, and let go of the past. However, when a new person, who you fancy, desire, have attraction for, and matches who you are, your vibration, your life practices, the things you love, your compatibility, perhaps your spirituality, and you have similar goals and desires for life, it seems like a fit. When your chakras are aligned or the level of awakening and development you have accomplished is a match to someone, it feels like you're in heaven. Why not take the risk, and surrender to someone like this?

Well, after not having been with someone in a while, it can be scary. It takes guts to your open heart again. It takes being brave, especially to those who have gone through such challenging relationships in the past. But once you have loved, the ability to love will always return. Sometimes you need a little push. And, someone who's a match is a perfect push to jump over that edge.

Have you ended a relationship not too long ago, and have fear of diving in with someone new? Are you afraid to get too close? And, if you feel like you're getting close, do you immediately start to pull away or push away as soon as it gets comfortable?

Letting your heart open is a brave and amazing thing. It feels magical, like bliss, heaven, and the feeling of a new love, a new sweetheart can be scary, but it also can be utterly exciting! You don't know the other person that well yet. You are in the discovery, the exploration, the journey, the ride. Let it be fun! Take the risk, and ride the wave of love! You might just land in the other persons arms, and be embraced with love like you've never known.

And, you do never know. The unknown can be scary, and it can also be fun!

**Section 4
Tantric Sex**

61 How To Turn On Your Lover

When you look your partner straight in the eye and tell them you want them, their heart may melt with agony and desire.

Gently touching their shoulder as you walk by and direct your energy toward them with love and passion.

Whispering in their ear when talking to them, rather than speaking loudly across the room.

Taking their fingers in your own, and kissing them, ever so softly.

Surprisingly holding their hand, while you are walking somewhere together, or in the midst of a deep conversation.

Placing your hands on their belly and pressing your hands firmly tilted upward, while standing in a room, perhaps a meeting, or somewhere where other people are around.

Sneaking out together and jumping in the car to a woods spot, or running to one while at your mother in law's house with your kids (leaving them there of course and where they are big enough to be left alone for a half an hour).

Spontaneously getting a hotel room with room service of all your delectable treats!

Laying on a blanket outside under the moon.

Abruptly grabbing your lovers head with your fingers brushing through their hair and pulling their face toward you, and then walking away.

Taking two hands each to the side of your lover's face and pulling him or her towards you and kissing them, so so gently.

Telling your lover you love them "no matter what!"

Making eye contact, often!

Moving slowly, often!

Surprise them with something they love; for no reason!

62
Sexual Power

Some would say that during the time of Christ, whilst he was still alive, Mary Magdalene was living in her Sexual Power. She carried the energy of love divine, was completely open in her heart, shared love with her Beloved Jesus as well as the love they shared with others. In essence, they lived a polyamorous life, and were free in themselves to share this love with each other as well as the love they shared with others in their life. There were no threats. There was no jealousy. There was no fear. Jesus and Mary were the ultimate gurus and teachers and leaders of their time and were very advanced spiritually, psychologically as well as sexually.

To be totally free in my sexuality is still a quest I am working towards. To be free in speech with all of my lovers of my interactions with them will be a reward I am deeply looking forward to. The ability to be free in our communication with those we love is the exact location where we receive our power. When we are out of integrity with ourselves about our actions or desires of our actions with those we deeply care for, there is a definite leakage in our energy field that could be fully embodied when we were free to communicate all of our affairs with one another.

However, there is also a correlation to having a need to speak with those we love and feeling safe, feeling as though they will still love us and gaining an approval from someone outside of ourselves. If there has been an agreement to be open, then the openness is granted. There is no further need to express other than this. Although, when both people in a couple, or all people in a love affair can share openly about their feelings of love for each other and their love for others, it creates a depth of intimacy not normally experienced in this culture. We have all been raised to be monogamous, and to share our love with only one lover; our husband or wife, however, to keep our power, to shine in our love for many is the ultimate journey for realization, full self-expression and vibrancy in oneself.

There are many fears that our culture has around this idea, as well as fears we each have individually. When we can shine in our fullness, and still love deeply those we cherish and adore, this is when we can truly shine and vibrate the passionate presence of love in our hearts. This is when we can ultimately achieve the sexual power we all are longing for.

I wish you love and liberation on your journey!

63 Unfolding Pleasure

What does it mean when you read the words "Unfolding Pleasure?"

Unfolding Pleasure is about the unlimited ability to unravel and peel the layers of our-self to reveal and awaken the joy, the bliss, the love, the harmony and the pleasure underneath. Our bodies are capable of continuing to release the blocks that we carry around ourselves. And just as our bodies can release these layers, so can our minds, our thoughts, our thinking process, our emotions, our hearts and our entire energy system. When all these parts of our-selves are cleared and released of the darkness held within them, we can then unfold the tight vessel and cocoon that we live in and awaken the butterfly of our true essence.

Unfolding Pleasure is an ever unfolding to our natural abilities, our pure innocence and our innate talents and joys as a human being. If everyone could feel pleasure all the time and be in a state of bliss and joy in every moment, then no work would need to be done and we would almost be walking as if we were a state of an angel that had already transcended. Everyone on the planet has layers to unravel, otherwise, we would not be here.

I welcome you to unfold your layers and be awakened to the bliss that is hidden deep within!

May you always know that your ability to be vulnerable and present to what you are dealing with in the moment, is the exact thing that will give you access to your own power and joy of living!

64 Erectile Dysfunction - A Common Phenomenon

After about a dozen phone calls of people seeking help with their personal erectile dysfunction issues, I thought it was time to do something about this, and write to you.

Many men go through a stage in their life that takes them off of their normal routine of a healthy sex life, and often it comes as a shock to them; not knowing how to turn things around, and sometimes go back to the way it was just the day before. And, after many months of feeling frustrated, mostly from their partner wanting them to be able to be fully erect and feel the full sensation they had before, they start looking for answers.

First off, I want to say, ladies, please have patience for your honey's. Sometimes they don't know the source of this and they really do need help. It is important that they know YOU love them, accept them, and can be fully supportive of what they are dealing with. #1 this is utmost of importance. It will help them feel nurtured, cared for, and in the end get to the other side of this condition.

Second, guys, it will take a lot of compassion on your part to let your women go through what they are going through given they were always used to things being a certain way, and now they need to adjust to the changes and learn within themselves how to accept your situation, and eventually support you to heal it. If this core foundation doesn't happen, this is where a lot of relationships start going under and can, without warning, walk a path of termination. This is not what I would want for you, however, some people can only handle so much disappointment. The good news is, is that there are answers and this CAN, I am telling you, be cured. It will take DEEP soul searching on your part, a determination to heal your inner self and take charge of the problem. Going to the route of viagra or other drugs is NOT the solution. It will only lead to other health problems later, but I can't make that decision for you. You have to.

So, guys, soul searching IS the answer. It's not the fastest solution, and it's not an easy one, but it is the most powerful solution. And, with Tantra and other Spiritual Healing practices, you can find yourself getting closer to your old healthy body again, and sometimes, EVEN HEALTHIER!

Sometimes the issue stems from one or more of these things:
Your Health
Stress
Past Traumas

Often when you have a health concern, this can cause stress. Often when you have stress it can be created in many ways; work, your closest relationships, family and on many occasions Past Traumas that you never even knew were traumas, but your body took them in and integrated them into a part of you, and now it has caught up with you. The most noble thing you can do would be to allow yourself to be vulnerable, surrender to what your body is telling you, and go deep within. Not every modality out there will help you. Just like food; some people like chocolate, some like vanilla and some like strawberry. We all have different likes and dislikes and our bodies respond to different modalities in different ways. The best thing to do is experiment. However, now that you are here reading this, I would like to say that practicing tantra, spiritual healing, doing emotional release practices and strengthening your sexual muscles will help. However, with a little guidance, a little push and a little practice.

Some other modalities I recommend are (I offer most of these btw):
EFT (Emotional Freedom Technique)
NET (Neuro Emotional Technique)
Matrix (Matrix Work - Core Energetics)
Re-Alignments

IET (Integrated Energy Therapy)
NLP
EFT
Psychotherapy
Breathwork
Tantra
Caring for your health and eating proper foods
Yoga
Acupuncture (I know of a couple really great clinics around Philadelphia that cost $25 to $35)
Getting Massage
and more!

Some reading material: http://en.allexperts.com/q/Spiritual-Healing-3882/2009/12/Erectile-dysfunction-1.htm
http://healing.about.com/od/ritalouise/a/erectiledysf.htm

If you would like a woman and someone different than here, let me know and I can give you another referral. Or, of course, you can see me! Good luck to you, and much much love on this journey!

65 Why I Love Coconut Oil

Have you ever heard of Coconut Oil as a substitute for erotic lubricant? Why would someone consider this as even a possibility? What are the benefits of using Coconut Oil?

Most people use lubricants such as KY jelly, or other such synthetic made lubricants commonly found at the Drug Store or Grocery Store. However, these stores don't know what the best naturally made products are for someone and usually sell the run of the mill company made or products that can made at a lower such with a higher volume. However, the extra couple dollars for Coconut Oil, has SO many added benefits, I wanted to write a specific post just for this.

What Coconut Oil is to me:

Coconut Oil is an organic natural oil that actually feels like magic when you place it on the body. It is made for cooking, so naturally it is something that is good for the inside of the body. But not only is it good for cooking, but good for your skin and your pleasure! The oils made of Coconuts when found as Organic Extra Virgin feel so unbelievably delicious on the body, you can literally moan with pleasure with the slightest touch just slowly rubbing it on the skin. AND, it smells and tastes delicious. I LOVE putting it on my partner, and then slowly licking it with my tongue. Talk about arousal at its best!

However, Coconut Oil, I feel is best used when giving yourself pleasure. Don't get me wrong, it is ALSO amazing when giving delicately and intimately with someone you care about, so long as you are giving them the ultimate and divine attention. However, when alone, and you want to give yourself love, treat yourself as though you are the perfect lover, and make love to yourself with Coconut Oil. I promise you, you will never have had an experience like this before. It forces you to go inward with its rich aroma, and as this aroma goes into your body it slowly nourishes you from the inside out. It actually is a very powerful healing oil and is used often in India for Healing the body. And, it is an oil commonly found in Tai Food; which I ABSOLUTELY love; a rare treat you don't want to give up when you're in the mood!

First you want to scoop up the oil in the bottle, as it is cold and firm from being in the room temperature. THEN, you want to squeeze it into your hands and let it melt on your fingertips. After it has melted in your hands, then it is the perfect time to rub it on your body. You don't want to wait until it melts too much, because then it will turn like water and will be too liquid. Rub it caressingly and slowly over your belly, your inner thighs and let your body feel the sensation of your skin touching skin. It feels like silk running across your body, and it is such a divine experience! Sometimes the sensation of just rubbing it on the skin without going anywhere too personal is fulfilling enough and you feel as though you are utterly satisfied. Although, there is more to come.

When you are ready to pleasure your body in more depth, don't forget to massage your chest, your arms, your belly, your hips and your pubic bone area. This helps stimulate your senses to help open you up to a richer experience. Then when you are ready to be fully satisfied, remember to move as though your breath is moving you. Don't try to rush or speed up the process; otherwise, you've lost the joy of the pleasure and satisfaction becomes like a 5-minute quickie. Take your time. Massage yourself with this Coconut Oil for 30 minutes or even hours if you like, but you will feel fulfilled and totally in love with the Coconut Oil, and yourself when you are done! And, at this point, you can't tell anyone you don't love yourself, because you have given yourself the gentle time that your body and heart really needed. If your lover isn't around to take care of you, that's ok. This is sometimes better than sex!

The Best Types of Coconut Oil:

Organic Extra Virgin Coconut Oil
The ones best for cooking!
Be sure to read the labels!
If you look closely, it may even say great for massages!

Expeller Pressed is also ok, but Extra Virgin is a little finer and smoother!

I have been using Coconut Oil is my Sessions with clients and myself the past few months and the experiences have been delicious!

66 The Cross Between Spirituality and Sexuality

Tantra is a spiritual practice, with being fully open and accepting of all parts of ourselves. The only reason Tantra is called Tantra is because it encompasses all levels of our being. Tantra engages anyone who chooses to embark on the intense and advanced practice to enhance any level you are in presently, and empowers and accelerates your spiritual growth. It is not meant for those seeking it to stay stagnant. It is exactly the opposite. Tantra is not about sex. Tantra is about love and embracing the light within you to intensify your ability to feel all sensations on all levels, but there is no way anyone can truly feel in touch with all sensations and be open to all levels of their being without doing the work it takes to detox and cleanse oneself of their karma, their stresses, their unhealthy programming, their traumas or past history of abuse. However, it is possible to feel a tantra awakening and still be unhealed of these past experiences. With awareness, anything is possible. My intention for you is to be fully vulnerable, fully real, and honest about what you are going through or have gone through and embark on a journey with me to explore all levels of your being and create an experience that will uplift you, enlighten you, and empower you to live life and look at life in a whole new way!

67 Viagra vs Tantra Transformation

"To love perfection is to hate life."

There are many sources of what is causing your erection to not be as strong as it used to be, and if we find out the source, often we can also find the solution!

I've been doing tantra healing work now for over 14 years, and it's amazing, but even more amazing is having added the tools of tantra, to my previous Reiki Master training, and Energy Healer trainings, along with Life Coaching and Psychotherapy tools. If I hadn't had all that training, I probably wouldn't be able to say that I can help someone with sexual dysfunction issues, or trauma stuck in his or her sacral chakra, or solar plexus, heart chakra, or somewhere else.

So, what's amazing, is that I find people who are on the fence with getting viagra, and have heard tons of horrible stories about it, and I stop them right there, and say, "Please DON'T take that stuff!" Too many bad stories about it, and way too dangerous! But what I do tell them is that I might be able to help. Most guys are looking for their erection. They wonder why they have gone limp, and often they are in a long-term relationship or marriage when this happens. Most of the guys I have had success with this are 60 and younger. The guys older than this, the success rate is less, because it turns into a health issue and then we have to address the health. I don't have as much experience of success helping it from a health standpoint, but I am learning and may take some further training, so I do have more success.

However, if it is psychological, mental, emotional, or an energetic or spiritual reason, I can certainly help! Often it is one of these. For example, if you're having trouble with your erection, but you've been in a relationship for a long time, most of the time, it is due to issues within the relationship, and we will move into

Relationship Coaching to discuss the patterns in the relationship, or issues that might be causing some distance. If you don't feel distant from your partner, and the relationship is going well, then it is an issue with yourself, something internal you are feeling, something you need to process and let go of, or perhaps something you need to forgive yourself for, or someone else.

Another example, if you are angry at your girlfriend/wife/partner and you are unable to get aroused, there's your answer; the anger. Perhaps you have suppressed the anger and think you can ignore it, but then your body is telling you clearly that you cannot ignore it, by your loss of arousal or erection, then we can get to work on processing the source of the anger. If your partner has been blaming you for something, or judging you, or not appreciating or respecting you for something, and then you go to have sex with her, and are unable to get aroused, sorting through your own feelings about how she had been treating you up to this point, is what will help the erection come back.

Another option, is if you have a pattern of losing interest in being in relationship with someone, let's say for 3 months or 6 months, and a year has gone by in a newer relationship, and the sex just doesn't seem to be working as well as it did in the beginning, we may need to address some deeper core issues around commitment, intimacy, and the desire for freedom. This falls more into attachment styles, and if you have a tendency to be dismissive or avoidant in your relationships, and don't know why you have lost your interest to be close, intimate or even sexual, we will look at the source of this. Often it is something way deeper than you think!

Another possibility is if you are still in love with your ex! Let's say you got into a new relationship and perhaps at your core, were not done grieving your ex, there's a chance that you still are in love with your ex, and the energy between you and your ex also is still attached. This happens on a psychic level, and we will then do a spiritual energy cleansing process I call Cord Cutting, to help detach you from your ex, so you can feel your own body, and experience your life from a fresh start!

To go deeper into this possibility (still being in love with your ex), let's say you are still in a committed marriage or relationship, and you decide to open it up and have an affair or perhaps your wife/beloved is fully aware of you seeing someone else, and your body is not a match for the decision you made! Your body, and your genitals, are telling you, that you are still committed to someone else, and you may have guilt, or a lack of integrity with yourself about the new relationship! Then you may be fully ok with dating, friendly, happy, playful, and can cuddle and even have great foreplay, but when the act of sex comes around, you shut down!

Massage and stimulation won't alter your bodies response to what's going on inside of you. If your erection is weak, or missing all together, the answer is not a physical stimulation, or even a drug that changes your physical reaction. The answer is what is underneath your bodies response. Our bodies are very powerful tools for what is going on inside of us, and whether you are a man or a woman, it doesn't make a difference. Your body will communicate to tell you what is going on emotionally, mentally, energetically, and spiritually. We are a spiritual body, and often the answer to a pain, or in this case, a lack of arousal, you have to look much deeper than the physical. You can stimulate for hours and days upon days, until your sore or bruised, but it won't transform the reaction until you do the real work; what's waiting inside of you; your heart, your feelings, your core emotional and spiritual self!

There are many sources of what is causing your erection to not be as strong as it used to be, and if we find out the source, often we can also find the solution!

68 Desire After Being Single

What happens after you've spent a long time being single after a breakup? I know there are many of you out there. You end a long-term relationship with someone, for very psychological reasons, and choose to be alone to get over them fully, not jumping into a new relationship out of fear of being alone. You are perfectly content with being alone, and don't choose to get involved with someone creating what they call a "rebound relationship". Your desire starts coming back, and you want to make the right choices with whom to be with. This is more a Relationship Coaching post, however, there are also elements of Tantra in it as well.

You have a craving for passion, and yet, aren't finding partners you feel aligned with, are not a good match, or perhaps aren't even attracted to at all. Perhaps you've become more serious, or want to choose more seriously, not jumping into something out of lust or sexual frustration. However, you also have needs. You are a human being. Needs for pleasure and desire are perfectly normal.

What have you done to take care of those needs? What you choose to do, hopefully is done out of healthy reasons. Some, I'm sure will go to bars, strip clubs, and some men out there even go so far as calling a prostitute, a surrogate, or sexual healer. However, those aren't always an option, and sometimes they are not good choices.

Going to Cuddle gatherings is a great way to receive the nurturing touch you need, and perhaps find a new play partner at the same time.

Finding someone who is willing to be a cuddle buddy, or be a buddy in general is a great solution.

Finding a friend who is a casual connection and there is an attraction as well, is a great way to support that need for passion and desire.

Perhaps you want to find someone who would love to do a massage trade is a good answer.

Perhaps joining a group of something you're interested in.

Perhaps a poly group, a swinger's club, or even a book club.

And, some like to go to events such as Om (Orgasmic Meditation) through One Taste to fulfill their needs.

Or come to a Cuddle YogaTM event I created.

And others like to just hang out with friends, looking for that special someone and practice orgasms for one.

Whatever you choose, know you are not alone! There are others out there too, and you can find ways to fulfill your desires in your way, and in your own style!

69
Slow Sex is Best

Sex, sex, sex! Everyone loves to talk about sex! But sex to one person may mean something completely different to someone else. To one person it may mean going out to dinner, having a few glasses of wine, and coming home to jump in the bed with their hunny. To another, it may mean to stay in, put everything on hold, and do it right there on the spot, spontaneously wherever they feel like it. And to another, it may mean slow foreplay, lots of intimate massage, then taking as long as possible *before* removing their external articles and moving as slowly as possible *after*.

Most people, and in particular, most guys, think the faster the better, but that can't be further from the truth. Guys, and women too, feel a peak of desire, and want to rush to feel some form of satisfaction. They crave the feeling of pleasure, get impatient and even become aggressive with their own body. They almost in a sense, are taking out that sense of impatience and anger on themself, for having waited to be intimate, and don't realize that the slower they go, they more healing, nurturing and joy they experience within. And, too, the slowness creates an energy flow, the chi, and taoist energy movement, that allows even an emotional connection to their body, feelings and experience to take place.

Sometimes, the slower, the more sensual and the more emotional. Often, there is no healing without slowness, no emotional connection, no vulnerability, no sadness, and also no electric orgasm either.

There are many vibrators out on the market, and many of them, have a speed that is much too fast to allow the person to have a true tantric emotional connection or healing experience. These 'toys' are targeted more for people who are unable to orgasm without them, and all too often, they over-stimulate a woman, creating a somewhat dependence on the toys, and it sets the woman up for being unable to have any pleasure or release with her own partner (or herself for that matter). She then needs the toy after being with her partner, and then her husband, or boyfriend, etc. feels left out, unloved, not included in her pleasure, and it sets him up to feel failure as a lover; which is probably completely off base. She just trained herself to received pleasure from some foreign object, and can't experience pleasure without it.

Guys, it's not your fault!

However, there is hope! Women *can* retrain themselves to slow down, and men *can* feel the satisfaction of connecting with his sweetheart and beloved deeply once again! First, I'd like to say, is that it IS possible. You first have to put the toy away. Hide it in a trunk, or the attic for a while. Try something different. Try slowing down, breathing, working with your own energy, your own breath, a gentle touch, and let your emotions come to the surface. It will create a spiral and circulating effect of self love, love for your partner, and a connection much deeper than two people experiencing a superficial orgasm at two separate times and in two different ways can ever do.

If two people in a relationship, are both desiring to be sexual, get close, but one is angry, another is frustrated, depressed, or experiencing anything other than love, fast sex often seems like the quick solution to connect and attempt to make all those feelings go away. But, those feelings don't go away, without acknowledging them, truly feeling them, being with them, and loving them into disappearance.

Slow sex, and slow intimacy is the only way to truly acknowledge your partner, love him or her, and create a connection that is worth experiencing. *Why rush when you can have so much more?*

70 Arousal as Energy Movement

What happens after a relationship ends, or you have taken an enormous amount of time to be alone? (The relationship might as well be over if that's the case). And definitely the case if your partner had a fear of intimacy.

What happens to your body after you've gone through the grieving and letting go process, and you're ready to start dating again, or having an interest in connecting with others after all that time?

What usually happens; is your body will start telling you that you are ready. It will have desires with certain people you are attracted to, or give you sudden urges and nudges to push you to talk to someone. But what happens when you're by yourself, and you are starting to finally open up again after all that time alone? Your body may have waves of energy movement, or jolts of sudden arousal. It may feel orgasmic, but then when you go to pleasure yourself, you may still feel certain blocks to experience a full body experience of arousal, i.e. Orgasm.

The arousal is your bodies way of telling you that you have gotten through most of the grieving process of your ex lover (husband, wife, etc) and it has achieved a level of balance, equilibrium and harmony of energy and wants to move to a higher place of joy. You completed the cycle of sadness, solitude and aloneness after the hard-core break up. You took the time you needed to rest, recover, release anxiety, stress and sadness from your previous beloved, and now your body has awaken, and it wants to wake you up to match how it feels.

It can happen anywhere; your kitchen while you are cooking a meal, your car while singing to a song you love, cleaning your home, reading, talking to a friend, or even meditating or taking a bath. When your body is ready to open to a higher level of pleasure, it doesn't matter what you are doing or who you are with. It will move and rise within you no matter what!

If you talking to a friend in person or over the phone and you definitely don't want that friendship to turn into something different, be careful! You may want to hang up the phone or leave the current situation to allow your body to experience how it's feeling. Otherwise, that friendship might just turn romantic *pretty* quickly!

If you want the friendship to turn into something else, and your friend had been waiting for you to be ready and open, awesome! Or, you are neutral and don't care if this person will remain your friend or turn into something else, that may be time to have a discussion. However, if you have the discussion on the spot, changes *will* happen almost dramatically! A more rational stand would be to walk away, take care of yourself, and then talk to your friend later after the feeling of sexual arousal and frustration has calmed down.

I've discovered a practice called the Deer Exercise for women and men in my recent search on this topic. This is a taoist energy practice to help move and awaken someone who has been suppressed or shut down for a long time. If you are no longer suppressed and feel the energy already excited, this practice may actually just balance you and help release some of the pent up sexual frustration, and perhaps help you relieve the sexual frustration a little easier. However, I find the Shamanic Breathwork and Tantra Meditations to be more powerful. Whatever you choose is your choice, and your body will let you know what is best!

Feel free to give the Deer Exercise a try. Who knows it might help! If anything, it will help keep your energies open and your body in overall health and vitality! Enjoy!

71
Sex and Sadness

How can you feel passionate and sexy when you're sad? How can you open up to your sexuality when you are grieving a loved one who died, or a family member of yours is very ill or hurt? How can you feel sexual when you and a partner recently broke up?

Opening up to your sexual essence is nearly impossible when major life events show up. Even one of these events can take someone down a downward spiral for months, but all of them at once seems like a Tsunami of change and where something major is happening to teach one a lesson, or to help grow towards greater enlightenment. I am talking about my personal life, and using it to help others. One of my dearest and best friends passed away recently, and her viewing was in fact on my birthday this year. It blew me away to realize how someone so young could move on. Her health was suffering, and even though she was much younger than me, she struggled to get to the source of her pain. She had a history of trauma and I spent many years trying to help her. My lesson in my relationship with her, is the same lesson in the bigger picture of all of these events (marriage ending, her death and a loved one getting severely hurt). The lesson is, I can't heal everyone! As much as I want to help people, and perhaps be their hero, I can't help all. And, I deeply tried to help her, but she rejected me year after year. The more I tried, it seemed the more she pushed me away.

It's amazing that right before her heart stopped, weeks prior she finally reached out to me, and asked for guidance on her spiritual development. I waited for over 15 years for her to be interested. But then it was too late. At 33, she moved on, with a beating heart that stopped, and her breath became silent. Perhaps it was too much for her to try to heal in her body, and her personality would not allow it. Now, she can heal on the spirit realm, and perhaps in a new body and a new life, she can heal this life.

The end of a relationship also takes a toll. It's like a death unto itself. You have to interact with that person in a whole new way. Grieving someone that is still living is a challenge alone. You wonder why things couldn't work out. You wonder why they refused to heal, or were unwilling to admit their own responsibility in their own choices. You wonder why they project all their anger and blame of things they did, onto you. You can question it over and over again, but mental illness sometimes cannot be figured out. And, when the other person chooses not to heal or get help, the only thing left is to grieve. Being their friend is a challenge, because you don't know when and if they'll try to blame you for their own feelings again. It was such a challenge in walking away this time, that I decided to write about it. And perhaps, write about the struggle. And, maybe it could help others who loved someone with a mental illness. It's NOT your fault! It's not my fault. My heart is as big as The Divine Mother! But knowledge and wisdom in how to deal with someone like this, helps to end the pattern of being pulled back in, when they put on a beautiful act of being nice again. I'll consider writing more of the story of this. Perhaps it could be a short story. However, the lesson again, is "I cannot help so much that I sacrifice my life away!"

And to top it off, my father fell and hit his head! He had a concussion with delirium. He had memory loss, but only half the time. The status is, is that he's getting better! I am deeply grateful he is getting better, and I'll find out more tomorrow how much better he is. But at the height of his fall, I was there. I visited him for multiple days, and spent 5 or 6 hours a day just sitting with him, waiting until he woke up, helping him eat, and talking and laughing. It was very healing to be with him in this way, and he would say often, "why are you crying? I'm ok!" But I didn't feel like he was ok. I said, "But you're different!" And he said, "But my heart is the same!"

And I smiled and said, "you are right!" It's amazing how alike we are, and how much we get along; 2 Aries and my whole life I had no idea how similar we are until now. I am grateful to still have more years and time to spend with him, and I will continue to grow in the acceptance and understanding, that I am NOT superwoman, and I cannot save and fix everyone, but a part of me, will still always try!

So, the point of this writing, Sex and Sadness....how can one be in touch with their sexuality when they are feeling sadness? Well, simply, they cannot! One has to go through the sadness, to get to the sexiness. Many people try to ignore their feelings, their sadness, their anger, or disappointment, etc and go straight to the sexual feelings. And, then they wonder why nothing sexual is happening! Well, the answer is right in front of you! You have to feel all of your feelings, the happy ones AND the sad ones in order to feel to juicy ones! Bad feelings don't go away by ignoring them, then they only get suppressed deeper. The more you can feel your painful feelings, the more bliss and joy you can feel when they move through you and release out of your body! And, the body WILL tell you when painful feelings are there! It ALWAYS will, so you might as well go through them, and not try jumping over them! There is a much greater reward in the end when you do!

"Instead of jumping on medication, for stresses, just FEEL your feelings! Then all that stress and heavy feelings just simply go away! But you have to feel deeply, and at your core, or it will only come back until you finally face yourself again!"

72 Sexual Repression to Expansion

How does one go from being sexually depleted, lacking desire, energy or passion to finally feeling their own pleasure again?

I consider the body as a being of energy, light and movement, and with awareness, and knowledge of what is going on inside the body, what is going on in the mind, how the body feels physically, and the energy surrounding the body, one can get access to how to alter it to feeling how they "choose" to feel!

That is a lot to sort and figure out, one might say! However, really, our bodies are capable of so much more than we realize, and we ourselves have the ability to adapt, alter or change how we feel at any given moment. We can shift our focus onto what we are thinking and feeling, by what where we choose to place our attention. So, if we can do this, why not alter how our entire body feels at any given moment?

Some call me an Alchemist, because I have the ability to do this, however, it is a fun process to figure out what is going on, what is blocked, and then hone in to exactly the path to shift one's physical sensation and reality.

So on to the subject of "Sexual Repression to Expansion":
What are you dealing with emotionally? You can take on practices to sooth your feelings, clear them or calm them down.

Where are the emotions stored in your body? You can do visualization exercises, energy healing practices, chakra clearing and guided visualization or meditation to alter or dissolve the unhappy or stuck feelings that are not filled with light, joy or love.

What does your energy feel like around your body? Does it feel heavy or dark? Does it feel mucky or clouded? Does it feel intense

like anger or a wall? Does it feel confused or sad?
How does your body feel physically? Are your muscles sore or tight? (and where). Do you feel tired, lethargic, or weak and maybe prone to getting colds (weakened immune system)?

Once you discover these 4 main areas, and whether some or all need to be addressed, you can go deeper into tackling the energies that are causing the repression. One area may take significantly more importance than another, and possibly need to put all your attention on it for a while before moving on to the next. After all these are done, then you can go into the specific chakras that are asking for the most attention, do some chakra clearing practices, movement of the energies, and work on releasing the weight within in. That's when it starts to get fun!

Once all the issues have been resolved, the chakras are moving, cleared and open, then you can go into the tantra meditation that will create expansion! And from there anything is possible!

If this sounds easy, try it out for yourself! See if you can take it on and create the movement you desire! And, if you need a little help, feel free to ask for it, and send me a message!

Lovingly to your pleasure and success!

73 Sexual Frustration and Open Marriage

There's an extraordinary amount of marriages and couples that stay together for the security, rather than the desire and love of it. Couples have children, they build a foundation of what's comfortable. They love each other, but the passion, spontaneity, openness to each other, and playful sex almost disappears. Where does this passion and desire for intimacy go? And what do they do about it? Sexual frustration often gets transferred into taking care of the child/children, work, career, and time to just simply rest.

When marriages have lost their zest and they have a love for one another, this can often lead to dependency on the other. A fear of looking outside the marriage shows up out of fear of breaking the security they have developed, the security for the children and the harmony and emotional balance of all involved. However, when YOU have NOT had your sexual needs met, in weeks, months or years waiting around for the security of your husband or wife is truly wasted energy. I can understand you might not want to risk the family bonds, the close-knit family gatherings, and the fun you all have together for the sake of the children, but there comes a point when sexual frustration has taken over, and your sexual self expression is completely missing and void that your entire life force has dwindled away.

What do you do to take care of your personal needs when they show up? Do you have an affair? Do you secretly date someone new, keeping lies between both the new person and your husband/wife? Or, do you have the straight conversation with your family and husband/wife and talk to them about what is missing for you, what you want to create, and the fears, concerns, and pain it may cause for each other?

The only way to solve issues between a partnership is to straight up talk about it. However, not everyone is comfortable talking that boldly, and not everyone is willing to take the risk. Are you willing to risk your sexual pleasure, vitality, life force for the sake of keeping something solid when you are not happy? Or, is having honest communication something that you might be willing and open to having? Despite all the criticism, complaints, concerns and fears the other person may have, can you be able to listen to them, hold the space for them, and be loving despite everything they might feel out of your honesty?

You might be surprised. You might get your needs met, and you just might be able to have it all. Isn't it worth the risk?

For those I love, friends, clients and myself, I say YES!

74
Sex and Being Upset

When you are carrying upset in your heart, be it sadness, making someone wrong, holding resentment, judgment or anger, sexual energy may be missing and at most, going into the act of sex will be for the wrong reasons.

The idea of sex is a very personal matter, and when there is any upset at the person you hold the most dear to your heart, it makes sense that the sexual drive may be lacking or absent all together. Is it more important to you to have sex, or is it more important to you to be connected to the person you love? What I mean is, do you find yourself driven by the desire of sex more than the drive to have love in your heart with the person dearest to you?

Perhaps the person dearest to you, you have given up on, or perhaps you have been resigned about something you are upset about and have decided not to deal with it, talk about it or confront it with the person. When I say, "Being Upset", I mean simply being upset. Not everyone is willing to admit that they are just simply upset with the person they love. They might find it more appealing to focus instead on sex, or focus instead on another person, or another activity. But when it comes down to it and after much time has passed, the reality is you may be upset with someone. Maybe you left the relationship all-together and are even trying to date someone new, but don't even know why you are 1. either not attracting anyone new in your life, or 2. are not feeling fulfilled by the new person, or 3. have no sexual drive with the new person at all. Consider that you just may be upset with the person you were *previously* with, and on many levels still love them very much!

If you are still open to the person you deeply love, cheers to you for realizing your love, and being committed to waiting until the time is right to work out your differences. Not everyone is willing to wait to work things out. Many people often give deadlines and say, "I will give you 6 months," or "I will give you 1 year to x," or "If this doesn't work out by the end of this year or next year xxx...." and what you have is an ultimatum, and ultimately a heart that is blocked and shut down, and incompletion with a solution with the exact person you love the most!

When your heart is shut down from the person you love the most, do you still have sex with them? What is your sex like? Does it satisfy and fulfill you? Or do you feel something is missing and an emptiness?

No one is perfect, and upset happens. You are a human being. We all have upsets. They come and go and then you work it out. But when you don't work it out, what do you do? How do you deal with your upsets with the person you love the most? Do you avoid them, walk away and try to resolve it on your own? Do you talk to your friends for advice? Do you shut out the world and pretend it didn't happen?

And when there is something missing with the person you love the most, do you know that you are actually just holding onto something, and upset with them?

Sometimes the act of forgiveness, love, and letting go of something that happened or how you are feeling about someone close to you is harder than many people know. Deciding to forgive someone, and telling yourself you forgive them, is not nearly the same as truly dealing with your feelings, unraveling them as far as they need to go, and then knowing 100% for sure you have forgiven them is a completely different thing! Admitting to yourself that you are upset, your feelings are hurt and telling the real truth to the person you love, is the first step in truly forgiving them, and when you can do that, you just might start to unravel your feelings and open up your heart again! And if your heart is open, doesn't it only make sense that your sexual drive returns, your passion and your state of peace and satisfaction? :-)

It is a true gift! And, sometimes we need an outside person to kick us in the head and open our eyes! And then, all the rewards show up!

75 Sexual Frustration and Anger

It saddens me when this shows up, but in fact sexual energy and the emotion of anger all too often come together and in many ways are merged as though they are one thing. Many times, anger comes before the sexual frustration, and in particular when a relationship ends, and one's needs aren't being met, sexual frustration and pent up sexual energy holds in passion. When this passion does not have an opportunity to be held, loved and supported, it often then turns into anger.

The energy of anger is so strong, many people can pick up on it from miles away, from a short or far distance and over the phone. If someone is not feeling fulfilled in their sexuality, perhaps solely just taking care of their own needs but missing out on the connection of another, anger can be the prevalent emotion one experiences. This one emotion can be the predominant energy in ones being and take over every single interaction one has. If one has the desire to control, dominate and manipulate situations to their favor, and lacks the ability for sympathy, empathy, kindness, compromise, compassion or patience, anger may be the emotion hiding and controlling you.

Also, anger shows up when there are unresolved issues in the past, and perhaps the person is not yet ready to face the past, look in the mirror of how they are really feeling, and instead wants to project all their feelings towards everyone around them. The anger can be easily sorted out, processed and dealt with, but if someone is not willing to admit how they are feeling, cannot be honest with themselves or you, any amount of talking to them or convincing is wasted energy. You cannot convince anyone who cannot even be honest with themselves, nor does talking help you as the person who cares about them. The best thing often to do, is walk away, and let them come back later with their own discoveries, their own answers and admit to you their feelings or experience.

Doing any sort of healing in the sexual healing world, can stir up A LOT of dark feelings, and go to a very dark place. And when someone who is seeking healing in the sexual realm is not willing to do their inner work, it can be a very unsafe place for practitioner and seeker to go. It can be a very vulnerable place for both and working together at this level must be met with an agreement, an understanding and a true willingness for the seeker to be the student, to learn, surrender to the teachings and open their heart to heal anything and everything that presents itself that is ready to come to the surface and heal.

Our culture, of 2014, in the United States is filled with many people who have a lot of dense, dark energy, a lot of fear and anger, AND a lot of mixed messages of what tantra means and even to the extent that people are guarded when it comes to healing themselves or judge themselves thinking they do not need healing when what they are doing is going by a misconception of what society has labeled the terms "healing", or "therapy" or "counseling". And, in fact, there is confusion with the term "tantra" itself. The term tantra, in fact is NOT meant to be a sexual word. Turning its meaning into sexuality has been adopted by the porn industry, and in fact, this has confused the consumer and the audience to its true meaning of yoga, healing and enlightenment.

Tantra all on its own, is a VERY powerful word. Sexuality, all on its own, is a very powerful word. And, anger, all on its own, is a very powerful word! Separating each word to define what each truly means, and help those who want healing to know what healing is, how it may help them, and how they have the power to walk into their own heart, to find love, beauty and joy!

This is my mission, and this is my path! I love all of you!

76 Sexual Energy and Stress

When your sexual energy is missing, there is often a reason. Perhaps your energy is going towards dealing with a stressful situation. Perhaps you are taking on the energy at work. Perhaps someone you love needs your attention and support, or maybe you are exhausted or dealing with something in your body that is causing your energy to give it its attention.

If you are at the affect of your surroundings, it will impact your energy in your own body, your level of stress, your vitality and your passion. And, also, when you are going through a health situation that is taking up most of your bodies energy, that too will deplete your sexual energy and cause your body to put its energy where it is needed.

Keep in mind, all of these situations are temporary. You have the power to purify your energy and come back to your vitality, and you have the power to regain your health, and bring back your bodies natural resources, gifts and qualities.

Don't push pressure on yourself to be perfect and have your ultimate natural sexuality the way it was before. Know that it will return, and you have the power to do so. And, your best quality is patience with yourself, love for your body and knowing who you are, and surrendering to the present moment so you can do your spiritual practice, your healing practice and your health routine.

What are you dealing with in your health that is affecting your sexuality?

What you are dealing with in your life that is causing you stress, anxiety or repression in your sexuality?

Let's meet together to do a spiritual practice, chakra healing and energy purification to help the process along!

77 Grocery Shopping and Your Sexual Needs

Do you ever go to the grocery store, and after strolling and going to the check out realize that there are other items you "still" need to get? I often go to the Acme to get my trash bags, lunch baggies, water, fresh fruit in bulk, eggs, pastas, crackers, frozen meals and deserts, and then trek to the Trader Joe's for my son's vitamins, nuts, goat cheese, orange juice and yummy yogurt and then Whole Foods for their delicious soups, organic vegetables, "my" vitamins and teas, juice for my son, my nurturing magazines to read, etc. AND, more recently, even go to the Co-op to get healthy snacks and more natural sugar treats for my son. That's a heck of a lot of different grocery stores to go to, and not all at the same time, but do ever find yourself caught in the same situation where you need to go to multiple places to get all of your needs met?

Just like your sexual needs, your intimate and personal needs, you can't always get them met by the same person, or at least not all the time. Perhaps in the beginning of relationships it may appear you can get ALL your needs met by your honey, but as time moves on, you realize more of who they are and some of your needs are better off met by others.

Perhaps your significant other gives you great nurturing, cuddles you and is great to relax with, but you also have a desire for great sex, so you may find yourself being drawn to others, and sometimes without your partners consent. You may have a best friend at work or that you talk to every day that you can vent, talk to and really feel heard. And perhaps you can't always get the massage you deeply desire and need from your Beloved, so you then turn to the Massage Parlor or Spa for this need. If you're a woman and you LOVE shopping, maybe your guy will turn you away when you make his request to join you, but you have a favorite shopping buddy you like to call on when you're "in the mood" to shop! Or if you're a guy and love to go bowling, have a "guys night out", or go hunting, your woman certainly and most probably isn't interested in joining you here!

Sometimes it's okay to get your "other" needs met by other people. And, often, it's nice to get a little break away from the person you see the most. It sometimes allows you to appreciate them that much more, and gives you a reason to keep the relationship going, because in the end, they are the one you love the most.

The Best Way to Get All Your Needs Met:

Talk openly about ALL of your needs and what you are or are not getting met by your significant relationship.

Discuss your other considerations for fulfilling those needs.

Make agreements with each other to have them fulfilled.
If you have weekly needs, find a day and time that they are suited best.

If you have monthly needs or bi-monthly needs or every six months, be sure to discuss them so it doesn't become your partners problem or that they don't become the blame for your lack of happiness, but instead, you are in charge of your own life!

If your partner is not supportive of your needs getting met, you might want to seek a Couples, Family or Sex Therapist to work them out. Otherwise, you might be questioning your relationship and why you are in it.

May all Your Needs Be Met in the exact time you need them!

78 When Your Hunny Just DOESN'T Want To Have Sex

Have you tried everything in the book to get your hunny to make love to you?

Are you calling your friends asking for advice?

Have you seduced him or her on multiple occasions with little response or wake up from them?

Are you tired of rejection?

Do they always have excuses and are NEVER in the mood?

Perhaps there's another reason they are shut down. Perhaps there are deeper core issues that need to be dealt with. You love them, he/she loves you, but the little amount of fondling, caressing or stroking of your hair is getting old. You want some connection. You want someone to love you deeply. You want a tantric partner; not just some 10 or 15-minute quickie. Where is he (she)?

You try playing with your toys, you go out with the girls (or the guys), you are ALWAYS in the mood and he just drops dead when he comes home.

79 For the Guys
Your Prostate is your Vitality!

To all those guys who have come to me for prostate issues, frequent urinary issues and inflammation of the bladder or prostate, this one is for you!

I was walking through the Health Food Store tonight and turned my head towards the shelf that had this tiny little bottle just staring at me with tantalizing eyes! I had been passing by this bottle for eons and decided to ask the knowledgeable nutrition clerk for some answers!

To my discovery, Nettle is a potent ancient herb for medicinal usage, for hay fever, allergies and to reduce inflammation of the prostate.

CHECK THIS OUT!!!!

"Nettle is known for its ability to relieve symptoms of benign prostatic hypertrophy (BPH), a condition in which the prostate becomes enlarged and causes men to develop problems with urination. Nettle helps men to urinate more successfully during the day, and thus helps eliminate another annoying symptom of BPH—frequent nighttime urination. Nettle keeps the body from converting testosterone into 5-alpha-reductase, an enzyme that causes the prostate gland to begin growing again in middle age. Taking nettle in combination with either pygeum bark extract or saw palmetto may be to be at least as effective against BPH as the prescription drug finasteride. Commission E also approves the use of nettle to treat BPH." (source: http://www.vitaminstuff.com/herbs-nettle.html)

ALSO SEE THESE: http://www.prostate-massage-and-health.com/Stinging-Nettle.html

http://www.botanical.com/botanical/mgmh/n/nettle03.html

You can also try eating lots of tomatoes! This is also known for reducing inflammation of the prostate as well!

I also give a nice prostate massage to your Tantra Session, as requested! A prostate Massage is good for Healing AND for pleasure!

To your prostate health, and your vitality!

80 How Girls Can Keep Your Yoni Smelling Sweet; and not fishy (and guys who want to help)!

Every woman knows that there is a certain odor that your body releases from time to time. Sometimes your body releases a powerful smell after having a passionate lovemaking session, and sometimes the lovemaking stops before it starts because the odor is so strong.

Men like their women smelling sweet and yummy; like a flower and not like they're walking through the fish market. It's a guys worst turn off when you get really close with each other and then just as he starts getting excited, a wave of air rushes over his body, and he gags in disgust, and instead of being honest and telling you he can't stand the smell, he gets limp and decides to leave the room without giving much of a reason or warning. He swallows his heart and slowly; with caution, leaves the situation.

"Hunny, I have a headache". Or, "Hunny, my stomach really hurts. I don't feel well" etc.

But girls, I'm telling you, you are in complete control of this situation. You can make him crave you, or be repulsed by you; it's your choice, but if you want to know how to make him want you every time you get close, do everything you can to make your body smell sweet and tasty.

- Drink LOTS of water!

- Go on a green binge, and eat lots of veggies!

- Go on a raw food quest.

- Eat sweets, dairy and sugar in moderation. The vagina takes in yeast products like a sponge. If you eat anything that will develop candida, your body will smell like a fish store, so do it in moderation.

- Cleanse the candida as a regular habit; take acidophilus and eat more veggies!

- Eat apples, bananas, oranges; any fruit will do, but stop when your body tells you to; they have sugar in them too!

- Don't eat too much pineapple or mango. They have the most sugar of any fruit.

- Drink Chamomile tea!

- Go on a detox regularly.

- Drink more water!

- Go to the health food store or book store and buy a book on candida cleanses, yeast free products, or eating yeast free! All women need this!

- When all is said and done, go please your man!

- Use Feminine Deodorant spray's and wipes as a last resort; but don't rely on them.

- Use essential oils for healing candida and drink more water!

- Just breathe; it will go away. It's all temporary. The body is made of 70% water, so if you just wait a couple days it will soon pass.

- Another thing for guys - if you're horny and you've had this issue for a while, get a nice hot bowl of bubble or pure aromatherapy water. Lay your woman down and rub her with the warm wash cloth. It will turn her on and make you happy too!

Guys, pass this on to your girls!

81 Venus and Sex

So, I'm going to get into a little Astrology here. When it comes to relationships and our sexual desires, Venus runs the show! We may think that its our minds, our hearts and our bodies that run the show, and that is certainly part of it, however, Venus is the ruler behind all of it.
So, let me share the signs.

If your Venus is in Aquarius, you will pretty much do whatever you feel like. Venus in Aquarius loves everyone, and they don't exactly like to be tied down to anyone in particular either. Venus in Aquarius likes to be free, they like to party, have fun, and be like a child always. They are a friend to all, and don't like to hurt anyone's feelings either, but they will always make sure their needs are met, even if they are attempting to make others happy too. And, in the end, no one can make anyone happy but them-self, and they try to stick to this motto. They are best with lovers who can accept them in their need for freedom, or they will move on to someone else.

If your Venus is in Pisces, you are the Intuitive Lover! You'll be easily moved to emotional connection, and your emotions will guide you to your sexuality. If you are in love, and your feelings are hurt, your arousal may be quickly turned off. However, you are a water sign, so if you have a lot of passion, a lot of water will rise and bring your passions back alive. Pisces is the sign of the sensitive lover, and they feel everything inside of them. They move often like water, so in order to keep up with them, its best to try to move with them. Pisces is the kind lover, so they will often think of others before thinking of them-self. Whatever the other partner wants, they will do what they can, to make them happy.

If your Venus is in Aries, you may be quick to decide to be

involved with someone, get sexual very quickly, and just as quickly decide you don't like them anymore, and not put much effort into keeping it going. Aries is a fire sign, and can get hot very quickly, anger, frustration quickly, and sizzle out just as fast. So, the best way to keep a Venus in Aries in your life, is to not make them angry, or do what you can to make them fall back in love all over again.

If your Venus is in Taurus, you might be very committed, sensual, and loyal to the core. Taurus is the tantric master, and are very grounded in their love making, like to move very slowly, are the leaders of foreplay, and can take as long as needed. They don't like to share their partners, and consider their partners their own possession, so they would not want to go out searching for extra lovers, even when troubles arise.

If your Venus is in Gemini, you might be a very talkative lover, you may love to laugh and giggle in bed, and be prone to making your lover laugh as well, or talk their head off and they may want you to "shut up" sometimes. A Gemini Venus would be a very creative lover, and more detached. When a relationship ends, it might be easy for you to move on and go to the next partner. They would have an easy time with polyamory, and less clingy or possessive than other signs.

If your Venus is in Cancer, you would be very clingy to your lover, not want to share at all, and feelings would get hurt easily. Venus in Cancer would have a hard time with polyamory, and may not even think of it. Family comes first with Cancer, and they may want to include their relationship into their family, and if they cannot include their partner into their family, they may not feel as though the relationship is a good match. Venus in Cancer in bed, may want to cuddle for hours, make love for hours, and hold onto their lover for a long time. They are very affectionate, sensitive, and emotional.

If your Venus is in Leo, you may want to run the show, lead the bed-style so to speak, and take charge of your sexual interactions.

Venus in Leo would be very loyal, and proud of their partner. Leo likes to be playful, child-like and innocent. They are kind, giving and selfless. They too would not want to open the relationship to others. Leo's are loyal, committed, and usually stay with their partner for a long time.

If your Venus is in Virgo, you may be the most detail-oriented lover there is. You may have an idea of how you want your sexual interactions to go, and be very clear they are the best, and if your lover does not surrender to these desires, there could be problems. Love making to you will be like art, very precise, beautiful and divine. You would be best matched with another Venus lover in an earth sign, like Venus in Capricorn, Taurus or Virgo (or possibly the water signs of Pisces, Cancer, and Scorpio). Venus in Virgo would not want to be polyamorous. They are happiest with a committed partner.

If your Venus is in Libra, your desire for harmony and balance overpowers everything else. Your sexual drive will most likely be high. You are an air sign and will be aroused through the intellect. You are best matched with other creative signs. Venus in Libra would be very romantic and do what they can to keep the romance alive. In relationships, you want everyone to be happy, so if your partner is not happy, deep down, you cannot be fully happy either. You will do everything you can to make all people involved feel equally loved, supported and nurtured, whether it is a one on one relationship, or more.

If your Venus is in Scorpio, you will be the most possessive, controlling and demanding lover there is. You will be prone to go down dark paths, and do mysterious acts such as BDSM, bondage, torture play, blood play, knife play, anything kinky and wild, possibly journey torture chambers, hand cuffs, all kinds of sex toys, swinger's clubs, or anyplace you can show up with your lover in chains, and more. Venus in Scorpio does NOT want to share his or her lover and will do everything wild and eccentric to make their lover happy. Venus in Scorpio wants to be the boss, and once you are in their web, they don't ever want you to leave. If you have an affair however, and they find out, their anger will take over, and they will shut you out of their cave forever. Forgiveness does not come easily with Scorpio, and you may be waiting a very long time.

If your Venus is in Sagittarius, however, you are the most free lover there is, even more so than Aquarius. Venus in Sagittarius likes to be the leader, but they are also the most detached emotional lover there is. They like to bring spirituality into their relationships and love making and bring a sort of transcendental enlightened wisdom to the bedroom. They love big, but do not want to be held down. They are best with a lover who can honor their power and their need for freedom. They need to be held to the highest degree of their power and freedom, and if they are not, they will move onto to another partner who can appreciate and honor this aspect of them. It is a part of their soul and they cannot be anything else. They are best matched with another Venus in fire or air signs.

If your Venus is in Capricorn, you have the sensual sexual energy of Taurus, and are also extremely tantric, however, the grounding of taurus goes deeper with Capricorn, and they are like ice and stuck like glue to their chosen lover. Once they have fallen in love with a partner, they want to mate for life with this partner. They immediately have desires of marriage, commitment, family and children. And, when troubles arise with the relationship, even after many months, they still keep their heart tied to the same partner and will work through any challenges that arise to keep that love alive. It is very difficult for Venus in Capricorn to share their lover, or move on, even when it seems obvious to everyone around them it is time to let go. Venus in Capricorn, in their heart, mates for life, and even if they have a new relationship, will love their ex lover as though they were together just the day before! (They are best matched with other earth signs or water).

So, find out your true Venus sign, and you will know who you really are in the bedroom, and all the lovers you have ever been with!

Inspired from studying Jyotish Astrology lately, after studying western astrology since 1984.

Resource:
http://OnlineJyotish.org

82
Choosing a Passionate Life

The Benefits of an Arousing City

This past weekend I did my 3rd weekend of the ILP in New York City. I never felt so aroused just from going to a different location in my life. Being in the energy of the city awoke my energy to the vibration of who I really am and what I really want to feel. My passionate self is vibrant, expressive, open, playful and creative and being in New York I was re-awoken to this state of being. My shakti and kundalini energy got aroused to its natural state and who I became in the brief time while I was there, was truly excited about life. Not that I was not excited before, but being in New York brought my zest for life alive and it reminded me that it is definitely where I want to be.

The Costs of a Suppressed City

When coming home to Philadelphia again, I was reminded of the differences of the city, and there are many differences from NY to Philadelphia. The food in Philadelphia is fabulous, the music is unbelievable, the orchestra and parks are wonderful. However, the energy of the city itself is quite different. When I think of Philadelphia, I think of suppression, a heaviness, a weight of dissatisfaction, frustration and a large amount of people who appear to be miserable or for the most part uncomfortable being in their own bodies. People in Philadelphia can be cool, but it takes really getting past their armoring before they will let themselves open up. And, even that doesn't always do it. Being reminded to breathe and let go in every moment isn't easy when you are pressured to go to work, drive in traffic and then come home to your family. It's no wonder people in Philadelphia are suppressed. There is a distinct energy that surrounds the entire city, and everyone who lives in or near it are affected. People can become bitter, angry, sad, depressed, hostile, disinterested in life, running to outlets to make themselves feel better and living a passion-less life.

Who You Are Is Where You Be

I am in Philadelphia, and my family is here, and I am not in a position to relocate at the present moment. However, being in Philadelphia, in many aspects I become like what the energy it is we are surrounded by. You become who you hang around, and that even includes the vibration of the environment you are surrounded by. The vibration of Philadelphia is heavy, and I am an empath and intuitive. It would make my light body turn heavy, and my zest for life get dull. And, I am committed to living a powerful, juicy, and sexy life, and who I really am is someone who loves to be fully expressed.

> It only reminds me of the openness in NY city and how much it feels like home to me.

Asttarte Deva Shakti Bliss

Awaken to Living; Tantra for Your Whole Life

Section 5
Professional Tantra

83 Boundaries in Intimacy

As a woman, a Goddess & a Practitioner, I have many distinctions between how I represent myself in my work and how I am for others. I am not here as a replacement for your girlfriend or wife, but I am here to offer Healing, Support and awareness to your own journey.

There have been many moments where I have been in session with clients, and I have had to move the clients arm, or tell them directly, it is not appropriate to touch me in my sacred areas, nor even try to kiss me and that it is not acceptable. There may be other Goddesses who play the role of escort, submissive, or surrogate, but this is not my profession and not something I choose.

I am here as a Goddess Healer, one who helps transform areas of your life that are not working for you and targets the specific blocks that are keeping you from fully experiencing and enjoying your own body and your ability to receive and give love to others in your life. This is my specialty. I am like Kali Ma, and am here not for you to take on as a lover, but to learn and grow with and transcend, over time, the darkness within yourself that is keeping you from your own pleasure, joy and experience of love.

Boundaries in Intimacy are just what the words speak; if you have a desire, it must be spoken of openly and communicated before any action is taken, and if desires or needs change, then it is imperative to speak again when the new intention arises.

You must always ask permission before taking an action with your Goddess, wife, girlfriend or Beloved, otherwise, it can feel like violation, force, an expectation and in some cases sexually abusive. Women are very sensitive to their bodies, and if no words are spoken before an intimate encounter about the intentions of the engagement, there is no sacredness and there is no trust. And at the other end, when you do ask permission, make a request and set a clear intention of your full desires, needs and how you want to create the encounter, full trust, openness, love and intimacy has the opportunity to be built.

Women are not to be taken advantage of, but to be loved, honored, respected and adored. And, not one woman is an exception.

84 The Energy of Love

Without the energy of love, intimacy cannot happen. Allowing the sessions to move into a space of trust, respect, kindness, and presence allows the love to flow; and in essence the intimacy can be built on from here. Without love, intimacy cannot exist. Without love, intimacy is false, and based on control or fear. The only way to move energy and connect with another human being and oneself is through kindness and the presence of love.

Many people try to rush intimacy or expect it to happen without moving their own energy, or the energy of their beloved. Intimacy cannot happen on its' own. It must be built upon, the energy must be cleared and connected, and calm kindness must be present with acceptance, stillness, and an open heart.

Many people have desires for gratification. They want pleasure and to be stimulated. However, gratification, pleasure and stimulation cannot happen just by itself. Gratification, pleasure and stimulation cannot happen without making an effort to work on the energy it takes to create the love that's underneath the desire and pleasure. There is no quick fix. There is no instant satisfaction. Love cannot happen without putting your heart into it.

All sessions are based on love and true presence. If you want a quick fix, or are just looking for sex, and cannot see the value of presence, then I am not the right practitioner for you.

I am Asttarte. You may experience feelings and emotions that are uncomfortable for you. When you are in my presence there may come an experience where you feel emotions that make you feel uncomfortable and you are not familiar with, or you do not know how to handle. As you spend time with me, I become your mirror. I may mirror different issues within you that come to the surface because they need to be released and healed. I am not here to judge you or criticize you. I will accept your feelings unconditionally. If I notice any anger, frustration, irritation, control, resistance, or sadness then I may suggest for you to do some deeper breathing to help you move into these areas. I may also suggest for you to do some emotional clearing with me. If you are not able to feel comfortable in following my guidance, and do not allow yourself to go into these feelings, then you may not experience the session to its full capacity or walk out confused and possibly dissatisfied.

I am an empath, and sometimes feel feelings you are experiencing, as this is one of my many ways to help you. I use this gift as my guidance to support you in taking your journey to the next level.

My biggest wish for you is that you allow yourself to be vulnerable with me, so that I can help you in the best way possible. My sessions are based on love, and this love may be all you need to experience true bliss within. I am a guide and a support, and I will always do my best to support you and help you in any way I can.

85 The Differences Between Tantra Yoga, Sexual Healing and Intimacy Therapy

Many people get Tantra Yoga confused with Sexual Healing, Intimacy Therapy, and Tantric sex. All of these have their own definitions and are all completely different from each other.

Tantra Yoga

Tantra Yoga offers the practices of raising the energy through the breath; without physically touching another human being. Although touching another can become a part of this practice, it doesn't come until later, until one has reached a state of awakening and bliss within oneself. Tantra Yoga is a practice done solely and can be a meditation of stillness and a meditation of movement. It can be done sitting, standing or lying down. There are specific practices used to raise the Kundalini and open connections to oneself, and Tantra Yoga is where one needs to start to begin to awaken to these energies. In order to gain access to the Bliss and Ecstasy of Sexual Healing and Intimacy Therapy (Advanced Tantra Yoga) one must learn the basics. However, Tantra Yoga alone can offer an incredible amount of bliss and ecstasy, and once one realizes this, sometimes they no longer desire trying to get the ecstasy from another they so often thought they could achieve. Although, when you start with one you can most definitely move to another; in the order and time you are ready. Tantra Yoga is more like going to Yoga class and sitting and listening to the instructor guide the student through the poses; however, the poses in this sense are different movements of the body and different ways of expanding the breath. It is quite different.

Sexual Healing

Sexual Healing encompasses practices of Tantra Yoga, however, with a Practitioner giving a Healing Service with the receiver lying down or sitting upright. Sexual Healing is not a series of learning exercises to practice as much as it is a practice to move energies to help you heal blocks of pain, numbness, anger, sadness or any other emotion that is in your way. Sexual Healing is a way of receiving the nurturing you need in specific areas of your body. It can include eye contact while you lie on the floor, energy healing or reiki anywhere on the body, massage techniques, and guidance on moving your energy.

Intimacy Therapy

Intimacy Therapy is a very intimate form of therapy and healing, and when one requests this as a session, they must be willing to be authentic to their own feelings within them self and allow them self to become vulnerable with their Practitioner. Often times, a client will need to come to the Practitioner for weeks or months before they are ready to allow themselves to trust the Practitioner they are seeing; unless they are already on a deep spiritual path and know within themselves that they are ready. Prior to Intimacy Therapy, the client will go through a few practices of Tantra Yoga and sometimes Sexual Healing before opening up to the Intimacy Therapy. However, in few cases, the client requesting the session will know exactly what they are wanting to address and heal, and Intimacy Therapy can be performed immediately.

Tantric Sex

Some Practitioners who are truly offering "Sexual Healing" or are only giving pleasure or release and not guiding the student/client into the arts of Tantra with the practices of the breath and other exercises, are misleading the client.

Tantric Sex is something you do with your Beloved, someone dear to your heart. Doing this with those you barely know creates an entirely different type of relationship, one set up as a sexual connection primarily, and not of the heart. It often sets one up for failure of a relationship and wanting a strong connection that never ultimately happens.

86 The Many Types of Tantra Healing

For those of you with no previous experience, this helps you understand and to better prepare you to be ready for the Advanced Tantric Arts.

It takes a very brave and committed person to take on the challenge of learning the Advanced Tantra Arts; and for those of you who have never had basic experience with Spiritual Healing or Spiritual concepts, that is where you will need to start - i.e. Spiritual Healing that does not consist of the Tantric Arts (*the basics of Tantra*), in an effort to be more prepared for Advanced Tantric Arts.

Tantra Practices Before Sexual Healing & Intimacy Therapy (Advanced Tantra)

You will need to learn the philosophies and concepts of energy, breathing, what the chakras are and how we can use them to expand our body and soul, body work for opening the flow of energy in your entire being, energy healing for clearing energy blocks or emotional stress, yoga and what the basics of yoga are, what it means to be present, how to create consciousness within oneself and to use your emotions, stresses and pains as a guide for your growth, what your emotional and mental blocks are, the value of working through them, some Spiritual Psychotherapeutic processing, what it means to be authentic, basic meditation, and more!

The main purpose is to prepare you to take the Advanced Tantra seriously.

Please Note: The gentler Healing practices are just AS powerful as the Advanced Tantra

practices and are just as important.

It takes a ready and willing soul to dive into the depths of Tantra, and Tantra is not just about sex; it is about the entire person!

The Basic Tantra Practices are imperative to understand Advanced Tantra.

Some basic principles will need to be practiced to get the most out of Tantra practices and in order to feel all of its benefits. Basic Practices and Advanced Practices can be incorporated within one session; but being committed to your growth over a period of time will allow you the greatest benefit and the most expansion than just meeting a practitioner once with no prior experience at all.

This is my way of being authentic and truly listening to my own guidance. I didn't come to Tantra as the beginning of my Spiritual Journey. I had to learn the basics for 16 years prior to that and trying to dive in and understand the multitude concepts of Tantra can be overwhelming to many.

Description of Tantra Practices
Descriptions of Tantra Exercises and Tantra Practices below

Tantra Yoga Practices; tantra movement exercises, meditations & breathwork

Tantra Yoga Practices

Practices of Tantra Yoga include over 30 exercises of expanding awareness, awakening bliss in the body, moving the energy in the chakras, full body movement exercises and breathing exercises. We will move into any of the exercises available to us and create a sacred session fill with expansion and love! This can be done standing or sitting.

Tantra Meditations

Tantra Meditations are done seated, working with the breath, the kundalini energy, the Kegels/root lock and powerful visualizations. There are over 100 Tantra Meditations, and each can be used to prepare the client to receive a powerful healing session.

Tantra Breathwork

Tantra Breathwork is almost the same as the Meditations, however, this can include meditations as well as more physical movement. This can be done standing, sitting or lying down.

Tantra Shamanic Breathwork

This is a very specific practice. It is done lying down on the back, with the knees up and feet planted on the floor. The main intention of the breathwork is to release energy blocks in the aura, and emotional blocks in the body.

Tantra Shamanic Breathwork creates deep awakenings, insights and emotional transformations to manifest and create changes that help uplift the spirits; bring enlightenment to oneself and one's personal relationships. This is an excellent substitute to Energy & Movement Psychotherapy and can be a powerful catalyst to therapy, a way of taking personal responsibility for one's process in and out of a relationship, and a way of creating harmony in your personal and love life!

Tantra Eye Gazing

A popular practice often overlooked - Tantra eye gazing drops layers upon layers of walls of energy stored around your own aura, and if given the proper focus and time, can allow deep healing, deep sacred and intimate connection to occur, and powerful blocks to be removed while speaking your truth of who you are and communicating this to the one(s) you love! This practice is often done before anything else. It creates a safe container of connection, trust and intimacy to be built, and without trust and intimacy; nothing else can be done, at least not successfully!

Yab-Yum exercises for intimate connection & healing Tantra Massage

Yab-Yum is another Sanskrit word for connection with the Beloved. You will often see statues of Shiva and Shakti or Radha and Krishna sitting in the position. It is where the man sits in the lotus (or Indian style) position, and the female sites upon his lap. The man lays his arms around the female's lower back, and the female lays her hands on his upper back. The position is done with the Tantric kiss (forehead to forehead), connection and clearing the chakras, the breathing of the kundalini energy, chanting the mantras of the chakras, and awakening the kundalini to connect to the beloved!

Kundalini Fire Breath

Kundalini Fire Breath is a practice done solo. It can be done sitting in any position, and in Kundalini Yoga is often done during intense yoga asana postures. In Tantra Yoga, this is usually done in the lotus position while sitting still. The Kundalini Fire Breath creates harmony between the yin and yang, or masculine and feminine sides of the body and harmonizes the energy within you and around you. It creates a feeling of stillness and peace all over and other words for this are called Bliss! The feeling is mesmerizing!

Sensual Massage

Sensual Massage is a Healing Massage used to create connection, let go of barriers, and open up to the awareness of feeling touched and heighten sensitivity to touch, and allow for feelings of euphoria and bliss overall. Other practices of tantra are often done to prepare for this session and allowing at least 1 hour minimum for the remainder of the session to be done on Sensual Massage will give the feeling one deeply desires and deserves! Other practices are often done within the massage to heighten the overall experience.

Sacred Spot Massage

Sacred Spot is another word for the prostate for men. This practice can be added to a Sensual Massage for heightened pleasure or can be done solo as a Spiritual and Healing Session. When done solo, it can be a very powerful healing tool for releasing blocked emotions within the body, and when you choose this, please be prepared to drink a lot of water and have plenty of rest after the session is over.

Sacred Yoni Healing

This practice is for women. Yoni is a Sanskrit word for the female sexual area and when offered by the Dakini this is done for healing of deep seated trauma, awakening blockages in the body, expanding orgasm, and offering loving compassion and gentle support for the woman. Sacred Yoni Healing can create a feeling of upliftment and empowerment in the body and expand the Goddesses awareness to all that surrounds her. This healing exercise is offered with presence and loving acceptance from the Dakini.

Mostly this is a practice I have coached men how to do this to their women.

Goddess Worship

This is where the Practitioner allows the receiver to give to the Practitioner in a form that would allow them pleasure from having a lack of giving in their personal life. It is a time to let down walls and guards in regard to intimacy, however, the practitioner may still have certain boundaries within this dynamic and also offer suggestions or teaching in how this can be done. Goddess Worship can include physical intimate touch, regular massage techniques, foot massage, hand massage, brushing of her hair with your fingers or a brush and gentle loving energy techniques.

This practice is taught as a guide for couples to give to their significant other.

Sacred Lingam Healing

Lingam is an Indian Sanskrit word for the male sacred area. Another word for Lingam is wand of light! And, in Tantra and Sacred Intimacy, the lingam is viewed as a wand of light always, even when one does not realize this potential within him. In tantra, the lingam is a tool for awakening the kundalini and can be used to expand consciousness within himself and his beloved female partner. The male must practice the art of tantra for this sacred connection and ability of healing himself and his female partner to be created, however, with the tools and practice, this can be achieved. The Sacred Lingam Healing is performed by the Dakini or taught to his Beloved wife or girlfriend to help remind the God/Shiva/man of his own divinity and power within him, to feel nurtured, received, accepted and loved for who he is. He may learn practices to contain his energy and hold his power to expand his orgasm for longer lasting love.

Please Note: This practice is for the woman to give love to her man, and the man to receive love from his woman. Historically this was a service that was only offered by the Dakini and only when it came from a place of no expectations.

Sacred Bath Ritual

The Sacred Bath Ritual is a practice to create a feeling of unconditional love, acceptance and feeling honored as a man or woman in the world. It almost gives a feeling of nurturing as an infant or child would feel, and the mothering energy offered can almost be transformed into a feeling of deep and unconditional acceptance from the receiver. This practice is often done to prepare for a Sensual Massage or Sacred Intimacy. It also may be done to help someone repressed to reawaken desires and passions stored within them, and to relive a fantasy or create a fantasy never experienced before. The Sacred Bath creates feelings of peace and relaxation, an opportunity to be in the unknown, and to surrender to the stresses of everyday life!

Sacred Foot Massage

Sacred Foot Massage is one of my favorite practices. The feeling of the warmth of the water and the bubbles trickles up one's entire legs and allows the body to melt away all feelings of tension and stress. This gives the opportunity to share loving gifts of intuition to offer energy healing, and sensual touch. The Sacred Foot Massage often leads into many other wonderful energies and creates a beautiful beginning of an amazing session.

Pleasuring Your Partner

This type of Session is often done in a Couples Session, where the Dakini, assists you and your partner to the feelings of eroticism and tantric love. This can be done as a fully erotic session, or a gentle session of love and intimacy filled with breath, eye gazing, gentle loving touch and massage. When a client comes alone, this is often replaced with a Goddess Worship Session.

Tantric Touch Full Body to Body Sensual Massage

This Session is a full healing and full body session where all walls, barriers, and blocks are let go, and no guards are keeping the session to move into a space of sacred love. Both parties must be fully comfortable and aware of intentions, and nothing will be performed without consent and without agreement. All sessions are done with loving acceptance, unconditional love, and honoring the God and Goddess in each other.

Please Note: This is not a service I ever offered but other practitioners have.

Intimacy Therapy

Intimacy Therapy is a very intimate form of therapy and healing, and when one requests this as a session, they must be willing to be authentic to their own feelings within them self and allow them self to become vulnerable with their Practitioner. Often times, a client will need to come to the Practitioner for weeks or months before they are ready to allow themselves to trust the Practitioner they are seeing; unless they are already on a deep spiritual path and know within themselves that they are ready. Prior to Intimacy Therapy, the client will go through a few practices of Tantra Yoga and sometimes Sexual Healing before opening up to the Intimacy Therapy. However, in few cases, the client requesting the session will know exactly what they are wanting to address and heal, and Intimacy Therapy can be performed immediately.

Intimacy Therapy can include other techniques from this list including:

Tantra Eye Gazing Yab-Yum exercises for intimate connection & healing Tantra Massage

Pleasuring Your Partner Tantric Touch Full Body to Body Sensual Massage

Sexual Healing

Sexual Healing encompasses practices of Tantra Yoga, however, with a Practitioner giving a Healing Service with the receiver lying down or standing upright. Sexual Healing is not a series of learning exercises to practice as much as it is a practice to move energies to help you heal blocks of pain, numbness, anger, sadness or any other emotion that is in your way. Sexual Healing is a way of receiving the nurturing you need in specific areas of your body. It can include eye contact while you lie on the floor, energy healing or reiki anywhere on the body, massage techniques, and guidance on moving your energy.

Sexual Healing can include other techniques from this list including:

Pleasuring Your Partner, Tantra Meditations, Tantra Breathwork, Sensual Massage, Sacred Spot Massage, Sacred Yoni Healing, Sacred Lingham Healing, Sacred Bath Ritual, and Sacred Foot Massage.

Many of the services above are no longer offered, however, can be taught for the couple to help each other. The services that are focused mainly in healing and opening the heart, energy and emotions are still offered for those willing to do their deeper work.

87 Description of a Dakini

A Dakini is a Healer who works in the Sexual Healing Arts. A Dakini is a female version of a Daka; a male Sacred Sexual Healer. A Dakini is trained in the arts of Sexual Healing and performs her services with highest integrity of the receiver coming to the Sexual Practitioner. A Dakini is not only a Dakini in her work, but this is her life. She is a practitioner of tantra and the ancient arts of sexuality, yoga and the breath. A Dakini can combine her gifts as a Sexual Healer with her other gifts of healing, such as Shamanism, intuition, and creates a space of safety, sensuality and love. As a Dakini, she can also use her gifts of ritual to perform her healing sessions and fill the space with the divine archetypes, angelic realm, ascended masters, and any other higher being she chooses to call on. As a Dakini and an Earth Goddess, I like to draw in my powers of healing, intuition, and intention to create an experience filled with powerful manifestations of what one desires to bring into his or her life. The word Dakini is very ancient, and there is very little information on it from India or Egypt.

88 The Gentler Side of Tantra

Tantra is not just about a sexual experience. In fact, most people in the US, and especially the East coast have the mis-belief that tantra is completely about sex. T*he truth is sex is only 10% a part of tantra and the other 90% is about practices, meditation, healing, kundalini awakenings, movement of the breath and the body* (and I'm not talking about sexual movement here), being authentic and in your truth (speaking your heart, communicating what you really want to say, doing what you really want to do at your core), yoga practices, and more.

I am here as a guide and I have chosen to take on the path as a Healer, and I have also chosen to go so deep in being a Healer as taking on the role of a Tantra Healer; which has its risks and its benefits. However, a lot of my experience has been with men who desire to "release", and are sexually frustrated, or have a sexual encounter. My job is in telling you that this is *not* what tantra is about. My soul is speaking to me and is now telling me that I need to teach all of you intensely interesting men and richly sexual men that you need to get on a spiritual path that combines the essence of tantra; combining deep breathing and energy movement practices to raise the energy up the spine which has the ultimate goal of opening your entire energy being; your auric field, your essence, your radiance and presence. This is not the sexual energy you feel when you have an orgasm.

This is the blissful feeling you get when you are alone; taking a bath and fully relaxed with no pressures and you feel filled with light and love.

This blissful feeling is not the orgasmic feeling you get

when with your partner, but rather the feeling you have when you are truly at peace on every level.

The goal of tantra is to feel so clear inside your heart and spirit that you get to a place where things bother you less and you feel better about life and about your self.

Once you've achieved this, or in conjunction with, then the next goal is to work through any blocks in your communication or blocks in the energy between you and your beloved, OR remove the "blocks", that is taking away that empty space that is leaving you alone with no partner at all and drawing in the powers of your being to create and manifest the perfect partner for you.

My hope is that through this path, you will sooth your stresses, mend your questioning mind, calm your nerves, resolve conflicts with your relationship, and help you manifest a partner that is perfectly aligned for exactly who you are.

May you always be Blessed and Loved!

89
Sacred Foot Massage

Bubbles, warm water, and lavender oil await your longing feet to be touched, pampered and adored for an hour of intimate bliss and love! To be touched, and embraced with kindness opens up the heart, clears one's energy, and allows one to surrender into the experience of receiving; being nurtured, pampered, appreciated, respected and offered unconditional love.

I love watching someone melt, and relax in peace, knowing they are in safe arms, cared for, and can surrender their true feelings. It is fulfilling to give the gift of love and be received with gratitude that they allowed you to help release their stresses, sadness, or anxiety, and opened their heart.

Sacred Foot Massage is much more than a massage. It is a full body experience of bliss, energy cleansing, pampering, and opening up to the greater gift of one's own heart, as the heart melts its fears, worries, concerns and stresses, and can relax into the unknown, as though time was nonexistent. A true healing experience in formed, and with delight and trust, sometimes one's heart opens even greater and tears of love release from the body, as the stress leaves and changes form.

The opposite of stress and anxiety is bliss. As the body shifts the stress, it opens up to a kundalini wave of energy flowing that takes over and manifests as bliss. Bliss is a full body feeling of pleasure, however, pleasure does not necessarily mean sexual. It can mean a spiritual cleansing of one's own energy center. In many cases, however, orgasm manifests, and takes over inside and outside, as deeper breaths rise, energy expands, and love abounds!

Sacred Foot Massage includes a consultation/coaching part of the session, discussion of current or recent issues, blocks and obstacles, and desires of where to arrive/goals to achieve. Then the session includes a hand to the heart, guided deep breathing, and then getting ready to soak the feet in a tub of warm bubbly water. Then massage is experienced on one foot at a time, dripping water to the rest of the leg, and massaging the rest of the leg. Then the other foot and leg is done. Often a blanket will rest over the upper part of the body, with a pillow behind the persons head and room to stretch out as they relax deeper. After the feet are done, deeper massing into the thighs is experienced, and then more of a sensual nature massage takes form. As the person surrenders they may experience full body orgasm, and as they come to rest, I may rest my hand on their heart again, or put my arm around them to allow them to surrender into the bliss and love just received. Sometimes it takes a moment to get grounded and integrate from this experience, so I will sit with them and hold them until they feel settled and ready to get up.

This is an example of one of the Spiritual Tantra Sessions I offer. There are many other examples.

90 How All Sessions Go

No matter what you're looking for, no matter what your focus is, your goals, intentions, or needs, or "program" you feel fits you best, we will always have a conversation and coaching part of a session, prior to anything else. Before meeting, we will have a pre-screening process to determine your level of spiritual experience, interest and what your next steps of spiritual growth are. Then we determine if we are going deeper into a spiritual healing session (which always precedes any tantra work), or if we are doing more of a Coaching Session, which always precedes any Sex or Intimacy Coaching as well.

Even if someone is coming for health reasons, holistic healing, general massage, or emotional healing (such as grief work, anxiety, depression, anger, a break up, a death in the family, a challenge with their relationship or their sexual concerns), we will still have a coaching aspect to any session.
If someone comes for Erectile Dysfunction, or Pre-mature Ejaculation, we will still have Coaching and/or Counseling prior to any Session, to determine if it is energetic and emotional reasons, or health related, and the best approach to take.

If someone comes for Intimacy Issues and is manifesting the wrong partner, we will go into Coaching, to determine what the pattern is, the history of all relationships, the types of relationships manifested, and the common theme of what all the issues in those relationships come up. We may do emotional healing or energy clearing to release the blocks to the previous partners or go into a Cuddle Session and Chakra Healing work, however, Coaching and all sorts of talking is part of the session, and is addressed in the same session.

Prior to any hands on or touching aspect of any session, spiritual healing work takes place. Often it is a meditation, chakra clearing session, or a tantra meditation, however, there are other tools used prior to hands on work that may be needed, but it is not determined what is best until after meeting and the issues that are important to work on. (And, if a talking aspect to a session is needed and takes a larger amount of time, and then a spiritual healing is needed after, a longer session would be recommended, or multiple sessions to get all aspects covered).

Sometimes Reiki or Aura Clearing is needed in order to do any hands-on work. Reiki energy helps moves the energetic blocks and frees up the space around a person, so they radiate a higher frequency. The energy around a person is often more significant then their physical body, and any layers that are guarded or heavy will need cleansing before physical touch and closeness. If someone's energy is too heavy, too chaotic, anxious or fear based, I will either suggest seeking solely Spiritual Healing (with myself or another practitioner first), or a professional therapist to do emotional healing work (or they can work with me on this level also if they feel comfortable).

Then after these layers have been addressed, we can move into more physical healing work. We will heal the aura, energy body, and spiritual healing, then move to Coaching. Then merge all worlds together, and combine a whole-body experience, of spiritual cleansing and rejuvenation, coaching/or counseling for deeper emotional healing, and tantra and intimacy for going deeper into joy, pleasure and love!

Every step counts, and one leads to the next layer of creating a full body experience of bliss, joy, and profound peace and satisfaction!

And even working on healing the emotional layers of a person, can certainly and DEFINITELY take one to joy! Underneath all challenging feelings is love, and no matter what lays on top, love is always waiting!

91 Knowing Your Intention

Knowing your intention, or how Tantra or Sex & Intimacy Coaching Can Help you!

Perhaps this is you: "I don't know what my intention is, and I don't know how to figure out what it is."

Here are some possible scenarios:

1). You are married and are feeling completely disconnected from your wife. You want to connect to her, but you don't understand why she is disinterested in sex with you. You've tried everything you can think of, and your struggling in your mind about what direction to take. You're feeling at a loss and completely disempowered in your marriage. You love her deeply, but don't feel as though you're getting through to her.

2). You are single and alone. You are feeling very lonely, although you are afraid of letting yourself be open to a new partner. You've been deeply hurt in the past, and you are afraid to be hurt again. You feel as though you tried as hard as you could and the partners in your past didn't appreciate you or recognize the good things you offered in the relationship. You feel fed up, frustrated, hurt and alone, and you are looking for a way to change how you behave in a relationship, the pain from the past, and your ability to be open to someone new.

3). You're in a relationship but are feeling completely frustrated and dissatisfied.

Asttarte Deva Shakti Bliss

Section 6
Tantric Prayer

92 To Cleanse & Purify Energy

This morning and most mornings I am finding, as I'm creating a unique synthesis in the shower, I say LA EE LA HA ILL ALLAH HU the whole time I am getting wet and wash my hair. Then when it's time to use soap and wash my face, I use OM GUM GANAPATAYEI NAMAHA over my hands and arms, my face, third eye, back of the neck, ear chakras, crown chakra, throat chakra, heart chakra, third chakra and all of the stomach, my yoni, and then specifically my feet, ankles and up my legs. I feel VERY clean when I am done!

Namaste~

Ganesha: Om Gum Ganapatayei Namaha

Rough Translation: 'Om and salutations to the remover of obstacles for which Gum is the seed.'

The story of Ganesha is found in the chapter devoted to this principle. But for your immediate need, you need only know that for seen or unseen obstacles which seem to be standing in the way of your progress or achievement, either specifically or generally, this mantra has proved invaluable. It has been used it with great success not only in India, but here in the West dozens of people have related to me their success in turning things around in their life by using this mantra.

http://www.sanskritmantra.com/simple.htm

"There is no Tantra without mantra"

"Ganesh (sometimes spelled Ganesha, but usually pronounced "gah-nesh") is also known as Ganapati. Being the son of Parvati and Shiva, he is definitely a Tantric deity. One myth is that Shiva (who is the highest teacher or *adi-guru* of Tantra) wouldn't reveal any of the secrets of Tantra to his beloved wife, Parvati. But she discovered a time when he would be weak enough to reveal the secrets...during sex! So, as they made love, she would ask him about the spiritual secrets of Tantra and he would reveal them.

Ganesh, hidden in the shadows, would write it all down. This is the metaphoric source of the supposed 108 classic books known as "The Tantras".

93 Buddhism and Hinduism Tantra Masters

I am working on integration of sex and spirit, in regard to Tantra, is the beginning of ascension. Ascension and raising people's frequencies; teaching those who are beginners the steps to raise their energy value and be a pure conduit for light! :-)

Praying everyday! Mantras........Tibetan Buddhist and Sanskrit (Hindu) mantras! and one POWERFUL Tibetan Tantric Buddhist mantra. I just discovered recently, that Buddha himself was a practicing devotee of Hindu practices, highly vibrational Sanskrit mantras and Sacred Tantra. So, practicing Tibetan Buddhists today, are actually closely linked to Tantra, as the original teacher of Buddhism (Buddha) was a Tantric Master, and he actually practiced Hinduism to become this! :-) So, whether one is a practicing Hindu or Buddhist does not matter. They both are working in the same energies! :-) VERY cool!

AND, also Buddha, as a Tantra Master (today known through Buddhism) AND Babaji, a Tantra Master, (today known through Hinduism), are BOTH of the same teachings, perhaps the same person from a different lifetime.
more to come~~~

Om Ah Hung Benza Guru Pema Siddhi Hung

I just purchased these mala beads and was VERY drawn to them. I had a vision I have worn them before, and as a deep Tantric Dakini, I know I have been a Mystic Tantric Healer in other lives as well. Here is my journey to drawing in a powerful Tibetan Tantra Buddhist Master.
The mantra:

OM MANI PEPI HUNG (Tibetan) or OM MANI PEME HUM (Sanskrit) are good for this, as well as:

OM AH HUNG VAJRA GURU PADMA SIDDHI HUNG (TIBETAN) or
OM AH HUM VAJRA GURU PEMA SIDDHI HUM (SANSKRIT)
or OM AH HUNG BENZA GURU PEMA SIDDHI HUNG (TIBETAN; another)

"The Vajra Guru Mantra is the mantra associated with Guru Rinpoche, also known as Padmasambhava. This is a draft translation of a treasure text which explains the Vajra Guru Mantra. It was originally concealed during the time of Padmasambhava in Tibet and later rediscovered by Karma Lingpa (14th century) who brought it forth from its place of concealment and copied it down on reams of gold. It is simply known as *"The Syllable by Syllable Commentary Explaining the Benefits of the Vajra Guru Mantra."* It begins with an invocation and then goes into a dialogue between Yeshe Tsogyal, the spiritual consort of Padmasambhava, and Padmasambhava himself."

"The great master, Pema Jungne replied:

Oh, faithful lady, what you have said is so very true. In the future, such times will befall sentient beings and both in a temporary and in a long-term sense, the benefits of the Vajra Guru mantra can be definitely be felt. Since my spiritual instructions and the methods of practice that I offer are immeasurable, I have hidden a great number of treasure teachings in the water, rocks, the sky and so forth. In these evil times, even individuals with fortunate karma will find it difficult to encounter these teachings. It will be difficult to bring together the necessary circumstances for these teachings to be revealed. This is a sign that the collective merit of beings is on the wane.

However, at such times, if this essence mantra, the Vajra Guru mantra, is repeated as much as possible, a hundred times, a thousand times, ten thousand times, a hundred thousand times, a million, ten million, a hundred million times and so forth, if it is repeated in holy places, in temples, next to great rivers, in areas where gods and demons abound, if it is recited in these places by tantric practitioners with pure samaya, by people with monastic ordination who maintain their vows purely, by men and women who possess faith in the teachings, if they give rise to bodhicitta on a grand scale and recite this mantra, then the benefits and advantages and energy of such practice are truly inconceivable.

This will avert all of the negative forces of disease, famine, unrest, bad harvests and all bad omens and indications in all the countries of the world, such that the rain will fall in a timely manner for the crops so there will always be a plentiful supply of water for agriculture and for human and animal life, and all regions and areas will experience prosperity and auspicious conditions.

In this life, in future lives, and in the intermediate state between death and rebirth, these individuals who practice in this way will meet with me again and again. The very best of these individuals will actually meet me in their waking consciousness. Those of middling degree of attainment will meet with me again and again in their dreams. Gradually perfecting the different paths and levels of their practice, they will attain to the ranks of the masculine and feminine holders of intrinsic awareness in my pure land in the continent of Ngayab. Have no doubt of this.

If this mantra is recited a hundred times a day, merely a hundred times a day without interruption, one will become attractive to others and will effortlessly come by food and wealth and the necessities of life.

If one recites it a thousand or ten thousand times on a daily basis, one is able to literally overwhelm others with one's brilliance, in the sense of becoming very charismatic and influential in exerting a positive influence over others, and one will gain unhindered force of blessings and spiritual power.

If one repeats it a hundred thousand or a million times on a regular basis one will become capable of effecting an immeasurably great benefit for beings, exactly as one would wish to.

If one recites the mantra three or seven million times, one is never separate from the buddhas of the three times and one becomes inseparable from me.

All the gods and demons of existence will attend to one and offer their praises.

In the most excellent cases, individuals will attain the rainbow body, and the final level of attainment in this lifetime. On a more middling level, at the moment of death, the mother and child aspects of radiant luminosity will meet. At the very least, individuals will behold my face in the bardo state and all the appearances of the bardo state will be free in their own ground such that these individuals will be reborn on the continent of Ngayab and from that vantage point, be able to accomplish an immeasurable amount of benefit to beings. Thus, the Guru replied to Yeshe Tsogyal.

She responded by saying:

Oh, great master, it is extremely kind of you to have spoken of these vast and immeasurable advantages of the spiritual energy of this mantra. For the benefit of sentient beings in the future however, a detailed explanation would be of enormous benefit, and so I would ask you to speak in a brief way about the different syllables of this mantra.

To which the great master replied:

O daughter of good family, the Vajra Guru mantra is not just my single essence mantra, it is the very essence or life force of all the deities of the four classes of tantra, of all the nine yanas, and all of the 84,000 collections of dharma teachings. The essence of all of the buddhas of the three times, all of the gurus, yidams, dakas, and dakinis, dharma protectors, etc., the essence of all of these is contained and is complete within this mantra. How, you may ask, does this work? What is the reason for all these being complete with this mantra? Listen well and hold this in mind. Read it again and again. Write it out for the benefit of sentient beings and teach it or demonstrate it to beings in the future."

OM AH HUNG BENZA GURU PEMA SIDDHI HUNG

See the remainder of this translation at:

http://www.rinpoche.com/gurumantra.html

"With such practices, you need to first have this thought before practicing: My mother sentient beings have been suffering for a very long time, life after life. I also have been the cause of much suffering myself. In order to liberate myself and all beings, I generate the mind of Enlightenment, Bodhichitta, and Shall practice the recitation of this Vajra Guru Mantra. (say this 3 times)"

Another great resource:

http://newbuddhist.com/discussion/3393/bone-mala-ethical

and
AWESOME http://www.buddhaofcompassion.org/benefit
NAMASTE!

Om Ah Hung Bezar Guru Pema Siddhi Hung

Bone Malas were used in Ancient times and in Hindu texts by Wrathful Deities; like Kali, Heruka, Samantabhadra Buddha, **the many forms of Dakini**, and others.

Sadhana Practice of Wrathful Deities

"In the practice of Sadhana according to the highest class of Tantras, known as Mahayoga in the Nyingmapa tradition, the Sadhaka, or yoga practitioner, transforms oneself in visualization and meditation into the Yidam, or meditation deity, an archetypal form perceived with pure vision, which represents a manifestation of enlightened awareness. By thus mystically identifying oneself with this deity during the course of the meditation practice session, one may thereby come to access within oneself the powers, capacities, and wisdoms associated with that particular form of Buddha enlightenment in manifestation. By transforming oneself into the Yidam and meditating in this state, the potentialities associated with the Yidam that are latent in one's stream of consciousness may be awakened, whereas ordinarily they are dormant and latent. Awakening into the form of the Yidam, one discovers that the deity finds itself in the sacred symmetrical space of the Mandala, which, during the meditation session, represents a temporary virtual reality, or divine dimension, for the Yidam's enlightened activities.

Wrathful Yidams, such as Vajrakilaya, were manifested by Buddhas and other enlightened beings for the purpose of subduing and transforming negative energies. Hence their wrathful appearance, but the core of their being is compassion, their motivation is Bodhicitta or the enlightened mind, and thus their wrathful appearance is only an expression of skillful means. Much like the martial artist, their minds remain calm and clear, and their hearts totally compassionate toward the suffering of all living beings in Samsara."

http://vajranatha.com/books/wrathful-deities.html

http://vajrantha.com/teaching/dakini.htm

Awaken to Living; Tantra for Your Whole Life

**Section 7
Tantric Men**

94 Gratitude for the Guys

After several weeks of going through my own personal journey of development, I came to a point of being really down and fearful I could make it through the hurdles and take care of myself. After reaching out, and sharing my personal experience, and letting myself be available, I found that my present followers, clients and network was an amazing support and was so open and willing to be there for me, by letting me give to them in session. I was amazed to know the sincerity and commitment of their love and kindness and their immediate willingness to make a change, so they could travel to see me.

I now have much appreciation for them in return and know, of those who see me, who is truly sincere in heart and devoted to me. I want to thank you ever so much for your love, your availability, your acknowledgement and your support. I also want to thank you for your patience, and your acceptance in knowing, I am still here and am also committed to you. As I continue on this journey of empowering myself, I know still, I am doing what I am called to do, and in alignment with my purpose.

For those of you who have not seen me in a while, I also want to thank you for being in my life. I know in your heart, if you were available and had the inspiration to see me, you would be here.

Some Questions to consider:

1). What do you do to honor and acknowledge the people in your life your gratitude for them?

2). Do you have a gratitude practice and what is it?

3). When someone gives to you without expecting anything in return, how do you respond? Do you give to others the same way, to them at a later time, or do you ignore it and forget it ever happened?

4). Do you celebrate the moments you are grateful, or do you let time pass you by?

5). When you are grateful, do you tell others about it, or do you keep it to yourself?

6). If you're not feeling gratitude in this moment, consider sometimes you were feeling grateful and go back to the people, community, or company you were grateful for, and acknowledge them. It just might make your day!

Thank you!

Just a little reminder that you all are very important beings and mean a lot to me.

95 Angry Cock

It might sound funny, but it is exactly what energy radiates from someone's shaft if he himself is angry! I don't mean being angry in one moment either. I mean, if his over-all personality, energy and mood is the majority of the time filled with anger, frustration, resentment, annoyance or even sexual frustration. When a woman goes to massage a male's genitals, however he is feeling on the inside, his deeper core emotions, his cock will feel the exact same thing!

The energy of a man's cock will take on the energy of his entire self. And, if he is desiring to connect with his beloved, she too, will feel the anger radiating off of him. She will feel his annoyance, and frustration, his impatience, his neediness, and overall anger beaming energy right off of his sacred area, in addition to his heart chakra, and everywhere else around him.

If his energy is angry and filled with these emotions mentioned above, often times a woman won't want to connect with him, or will have a difficult time, because that energy is not a welcoming feeling. That energy actually pushes people away in the opposite direction, probably the opposite too of what he wishes they would do. An angry cock feels toxic, heavy and the opposite of loving; exactly what women desire to feel. And, if he is trying to connect to a woman, the best way to go about it, is for him to clear his angry energy first.

How Do You Clear Your Angry Cock?

The first step is to acknowledge that you might be angry. Even, if the majority of the time you think you are pretty peaceful, consider, that its possible your energy is not as peaceful as you think.

It's possible that your cock is not angry, however, it still may have stress-filled energy around it that is causing the people, or person, in your life to have a certain reaction. And, even if that reaction is that she cannot orgasm or orgasms very little, that too is an indication that your energy is not as pure as your lover needs it to be.

The next step after acknowledging that your cock, and whole energy being, might have a certain frequency that is causing women around you to have a certain reaction, is to do your personal work.

How do you do that? The term processing might be overrated, but that's one practice that is helpful. Find someone to talk to about your feelings, get it out in the open, and stop trying to deal with the stuff in your life all alone!

The next thing would be to take on spiritual or peace inducing practices; such as meditation, yoga, tai chi, chi gong, acupuncture, walks in nature, baths, drinking tea, etc.
Beyond this is to get a massage, but not just for the sexual frustration; the whole gamut! Get a massage, or energy healing session to release pent up energy in your entire being; your neck, shoulders, chest, back, hips, thighs, calves, hamstrings, arms, hands, feet, ankles, etc. And, when it's time to remove pent up energy in your genitals, do it with consciousness, not with any intention to release an orgasm (not for a while at least), and remove any blocked energy of anger around your shaft.

This post is not just for women guys! It's for men to truly get your woman and help yourself so that you can clear and open yourself to be a match for what she desires; the authentic loving you she desired when you first met, those many moons ago!

So, clear your energy and your cock feels peaceful, loving, and ultimately *sexy*! Isn't that what you want your loved one(s) to feel from you anyway?

Asttarte Deva Shakti Bliss

Awaken to Living; Tantra for Your Whole Life

Section 8
Tantric Asttarte

96
A True Tantrikas Journey

If you are truly on the path of tantra, you will not find it an easy journey. It is actually the most challenging, difficult and psychologically draining journey you could ever possibly travel on. You go from the absolute extreme emotions of utter bliss, ecstasy, full body whales of sighing passion to the deepest and most dark places of sadness, gloom, misery, depression, releasing whatever and wherever emotions that have been pulled up from the deepest core inside of yourself.

It took me 5 years of being on this Tantra Path to put words to this journey, but a warning or perhaps a reminder, that this is, if you choose to truly embark on the depth of what tantra offers you, the most challenging journey you could travel.

(Meaning if you truly do the tantra practices exactly as they are meant to be done. There are milder versions of them if you are not ready, which I teach as well, but being a Goddess and Tantra Practitioner, I don't play small. I dive in and do them exactly as they are meant to be done. Yes, I used to have that old sticker on my car as a teenager and young 20s girl NO FEAR! Well, you literally have to have No Fear when you dive into Tantra, because diving into tantra IS like diving into the deep end of a pool, your own pool that is of your own self; the shadow self of the unconscious mind.)

I was in this blissful place over the summer. I was feeling really good, excited about life, making goals and starting to work on them (i.e. one of them was to start a Tantra Community here in Philadelphia with a huge list of details to go underneath it to make it happen). I was in the SELP course through Landmark Education. I was doing my private sessions to the best of my ability with a 3 day a week schedule from taking care of my toddler half the week. I was pretty much high on life. And, then, all of a sudden, I made a drastic decision. I decided to go to my semi-annual Tantra Community event with my tantra family. We met in NY in the middle of nowhere, 2 hours west of the city, at this bed and breakfast place. There was about 35 or 40 people total at this event. It was pretty cold, and few wanted to drive (I was one of maybe 4 or five people who drove), and the rest took a shuttle bus from NY city. Some flew in from out West; actually, most flew in from AZ, CA, and other places in the US. But this is my tantra family, or what I consider my tantra family, and I wanted to be with them.

The cat that threw my reality off kilter was my beloved, amazing that is, Tantra Teacher & Practitioner, Lawrence Lanoff. This guy is one of the most evolved men I have met on this planet. Talk about wisdom and transformation. If you want to change anything in your life and throw yourself into a gutter of darkness to face whatever patterns have kept you from avoiding the reason why you are miserable or frustrated in your current situation; this guy will throw you off your rocker and turn your whole world around. That's what he did for me; in the mildest of expressions!!!! I did a breathwork exercise with him in NY, many years ago. And, every time I went to a Conference, he led a new breathwork exercise I learned at the conference, often in Sedona, AZ in the spring and somewhere on the East Coast in the fall. And, he blows my mind; literally. Now, what's good is that I can take these teachings and then turn them over and teach them all to you, which I have done over the years, but this time, his teaching, and my taking it on, threw me in a whirlwind, of the deepest depression I have ever been in my life. I went into my own darkness. It's the core of the pit of your own armoring that is carrying your body frame in its particular way of holding patterns, the way you walk, your mannerisms, the way you stand and hold your posture, the way your head turns on a certain angle and how you look at the world and how the world then looks at you. ALL OF THIS, LET ME TELL YOU COMPLETELY CHANGES FROM WORKING WITH THIS MAN!!!

I then did my powerful Tantra Breathwork, which I call Tantra Psychotherapy, practices of Tantra I learned from <u>Laurie Handlers</u>, many years ago, to release all of the deep emotions that came up from Lawrence Lanoff's powerful tantra breathwork exercise. Now, each of the breathing exercises are COMPLETELY different, and they all do completely different things!!! How do you compute that? Well, if you really tried it, you would know what I'm talking about!!! So, I used Laurie's <u>Butterfly Workshops</u> Tantra exercises to release what came up (rage, sadness, depression, sorrow, misery, confusion, paranoia, etc), which took about 2 months of doing all these practices religiously and then 3 days ago did <u>Lawrence Lanoff's</u> powerful breathing practice again, and WHAMMMM, would you know, I am feeling wildly passionate, energetic and open as ever again. Like the tiger prowess coming back to life. This Tantra path makes you think you have some serious emotional issues, but in actuality, what it does it remove those serious emotional feelings that cause you to live in a rut and unhappy with your life. They appear to be even more powerful than Psychotherapy itself, but I will not negate psychotherapy at all; however, the combination is mind blowing, and if your heart is closed, you are living in fear, have some scars from abuse, or frustrated in a relationship, and you take tantra to heart, and truly use the practices to help you, it will not only help you. It will liberate your entire body, and your entire soul!

God Bless You, and I hope for you that you do the practices to empower yourself but be sure to have a practitioner by your side, at the phone, or contact in any way you can for support while your life shows up in your face and makes you look at yourself at what you have been covering for years. You can heal your whole life with Tantra. I am living proof of that!

I am now back, alive, open, awake in my heart, body and soul! And, it feels damn good to be here!

97
Remembering Presence

During the moments of quiet within each breath and the whispers of every second, remaining still becomes presence, and holding space is all that is. As I sit and hold space for my clients, I remember how tranquil and beautiful it feels to be still and present. And in time in sessions this beauty and presence feels like it could last for eternity. Being present is a meditation and a joy to achieve, and although it sounds simple to attain, for many it can be very difficult. And so, this is where tantra practice comes in to achieve this balance and doing this with another allows the attainment that much easier. Offering the sessions to another allows the mirror to be reflected; the love you put out comes back to you, the peace you put out comes back to you, and the presence you put out comes back you. Anything you give is received and offered back as love. And so, in being still, we create this miracle together.

It has been a couple months since I've offered sessions from after the birth of my beautiful baby. As I return to my practice and the sacred art of healing, by giving of service through sessions, I return to what I love and remember the beauty of being still. As I give to others, I also receive and in teaching meditation and love to others, I also reach the still place of meditation and love in my own self. This gift of giving can be a miracle; not only the miracle of healing to others, but also the miracle of healing oneself.

I only know the depth and immensity of what healing can do for others by how deep it has impacted my own life. My own testimony to how much I have transformed from all healing paths that I have been trained, received healing, and have had experience in some way is the only way that I know how intensely powerful they all are. However, you must be truly willing to delve deep inside in order to come out of your own shell like the butterfly blossoms from its cocoon.

As we become still in moments that feel challenging to slow down our body, and slow down our mind, this is when we can truly transform and open our hearts to a more serene place of love. And in being present to others we are also present to ourselves. And, in Tantra, this is healing in a universal way; helping the self and helping the other as the circle of energy makes its way around; from you into them, from them into you and continues this cycle again and again until you choose to end the practice. The energy cycles and circulates from one to another and presence remains while love grows stronger and healing blossoms from within. There is nothing more beautiful and miraculous than this. Slowing down is the biggest key to healing; whether it is tantric healing or any other form; practicing presence is all you need.

98 Psychic Sexual Healer

It stumbled upon me today that there is a deep connection between my sessions of Tantric Healing and that of being an empath. I don't know if you know this, or perhaps don't quite understand the depth of it, but I am an empath. Other words for an empath are intuitive or psychic. An empath is someone who feels other's pains; by usually feeling the same exact pain in their own body as you do in yours.

Examples: If you have a headache, often I will feel a pulsing sensation in my head on or close to the area of your headache, or if you have a broken heart, I may feel a tingling sensation in my own heart, or if your legs are tight and cramping, I may feel a heavy weight and pressure on my legs while I am sitting close to you.

Before embarking on this intense path of tantra and sacred sexual healing, my focus was only on the intuitive healing side of this new age phenomenon of healing. However, I have chosen to open myself up to the more vulnerable energies of sexuality, and in this there are risks.

The risks of being in this work, as a Healer, is that I become a sponge and take on other people stresses, just by them being in my presence. I don't have to do anything. I just sit with you, be with you, and can sense where your stress is, where your pain is, where your body is hurting, if your heart is hurting, if you have a headache, if your legs are cramping, if you are uncomfortable, and if you are going through turmoil in your personal life, or have had trauma in the past. I can even feel if you are anxious, stressed, or nervous being in my presence. However, the advantages of this is that I move into your space at the level I feel you are ready, and do not push you into doing anything you are not comfortable with. And also, will protect my space if I sense you are trying to dive into mine too quickly.

The point of all of this is that being an empath, and taking on others stresses and pains, I have to cleanse my energy quite often so that I can be a clear vessel of light, love and healing for the next person. I also cannot open myself up at the level some of you may want me to right away, because I feel where you are shut down, and guarded, and your ego or personality is perhaps trying to push through the stress you are feeling and unintentionally pretend it does not exist by releasing sexual tension.

I can only open as much as you are open, and if you are carrying pain or are armored, the best thing I can do for you is to help you open up where you are guarded so I can then get to the point of your intention in working with me, in a tantric and full body expansion of love and bliss.

However, that love, and bliss cannot be experienced until the weight on your shoulders and the energy imbalances and blocks are removed and cleansed away.

This involves tantric energy clearing practices, emotional release work, chakra balancing or other energy clearing practices, breathing and being present to the blocked energy, getting in touch with the pain or block you are feeling, and in a sense letting it breathe so it can release and move on. These practices can be done while in the presence of receiving a session or can be done on their own.

Asttarte Deva Shakti Bliss

The more open, expansive, and connected you are to the divine and living a spiritual life, the deeper of a connection I can create with you, and hence, the more I will be able to support you and help you in your desires.

With love, light, and awareness!

99
Practice Based on Love

Without the energy of love, intimacy cannot happen. Allowing the practice to move into a space of trust, respect, kindness, and presence allows the love to flow; and in essence the intimacy can be built on from here. Without love, intimacy cannot exist. Without love, intimacy is false, and based on control or fear. The only way to move energy and connect with another human being and oneself is through kindness and the presence of love.

Many people try to rush intimacy or expect it to happen without moving their own energy, or the energy of their beloved. Intimacy cannot happen on its' own. It must be built upon, the energy must be cleared and connected, and calm kindness must be present with acceptance, stillness, and an open heart.

Many people have desires for gratification. They want pleasure and to be stimulated. However, gratification, pleasure and stimulation cannot happen just by itself. Gratification, pleasure and stimulation cannot happen without making an effort to work on the energy it takes to create the love that's underneath the desire and pleasure. There is no quick fix. There is no instant satisfaction. Love cannot happen without putting your heart into it.

All practices are based on love and true presence. If you want a quick fix, or are looking for sex, and cannot see the value of presence, then you are looking in the wrong direction.

I am Asttarte. You may experience feelings and emotions that are uncomfortable for you. When you are in my presence there may come an experience where you feel emotions that make you feel uncomfortable and you are not familiar with, or you do not know how to handle. As you spend time with me, I become your mirror. I may mirror different issues within you that come to the surface because they need to be released and healed. I am not here to judge you or criticize you. I will accept your feelings unconditionally. If I notice any anger, frustration, irritation, control, resistance, or sadness then I may suggest for you to do some deeper breathing to help you move into these areas. I may also suggest for you to do some emotional clearing with me. If you are not able to feel comfortable in following my guidance, and do not allow yourself to go into these feelings, then you may not experience the session to its full capacity or walk out confused and possibly dissatisfied.

I am an empath and sometimes feel feelings you are experiencing, as this is one of my many ways to help you. I use this gift as my guidance to support you in taking your journey to the next level.

My biggest wish for you is that you allow yourself to be vulnerable with me, so that I can help you in the best way possible. My practice is based on love, and this love may be all you need to experience true bliss within. I am a guide and a support, and I will always do my best to support you and help you in any way I can.

100
A Little About Me & Some Thoughts

- I'm a total Sandra Bullock fan! She's a Leo with a moon in Taurus. Totally hysterical!
- I also love Jennifer Aniston, Sex and the City, Diane Keaton, Bette Midler, Kate Hudson, Ryan Reynolds, Ben Stiller, Ben Affleck, Hugh Grant, Patrick Dempsey, Colin Firth, Renee Zellweger, Adam Sandler, Reese Witherspoon, Isla Fisher, John Cusack, Meet the Fockers, any movie on magic and anything funny (I mean REALLY funny ~ No dark humor please).
- I love Sci-Fi, Humor, Romance, Adventure and loads of kid's movies! (Yes, my son and I do have a blast together!)
- I can't really stand living in Philadelphia, but I've been here forever (I'd much rather be in NY or somewhere else). Although, I'm very close with my family and I'm lucky to have them.
- It really irks me when clients schedule and then casually cancel. I'm not rich and I often have very little money in my pocket doing this work, so do me a favor and DON'T cancel! I don't request a deposit but someday I might, so please follow through on what you say. I can understand that it probably upsets others that I don't check my voicemail religiously and those of you that are waiting I'm sorry. I suppose I deserve that.
- I love being a mom AND I can't stand it!
- If it wasn't for spending the past 15 years healing my childhood and having been raped and all that (which I have COMPLETELY healed by the way), I'd be pursuing my childhood dream of being an actress instead of this, but perhaps someday I can be both!

- I have 3 brothers that I love and am very close to and I sometimes have to tone down what I promote online to make them happy (as well as some other family members). I try to keep everyone happy, but it isn't always easy.
- I, on the other hand, would prefer having sex every day and 2 to 3 times a week I would be very content.
- I'm not shocked by much. I've heard it all.
- I love beautiful and powerful women (as *much* as I love sexy and powerful men).
- The funnier the better!
- Yes, I do love to write, but I also love to sing, dance, make art and be outdoors!
- I prefer to be with groups of people, but I'm often alone.
- I love doing these sessions, but only when people want them.
- If you have a question, ask me!
- I love all people; even those that sometimes drive me nuts!
- I love learning and I will probably always take new classes, except when I'm teaching.
- Sex is really important to me, and so are a lot of other things.
- I believe in miracles!
- I love seeing children laugh. And, I can't stand seeing rageful parents with kids!
- I love it when you are willing to cry. It shows me you are strong.
- Anything is possible if you believe!
- Love is always there underneath any feeling, even if you can't see it and think it doesn't exist.
- Most people are more afraid of showing love than fear.
- I have a positive outlook on life and believe in the good of mankind.
- I'd rather watch happy news than all the negative. Although, it's sometimes important to talk about negative things that are going on in the world, don't dwell on it!
- I believe any relationship troubles can be resolved, but only if BOTH people are willing to work through them.
- Everyone deserves to have great sex. And no sex is sometimes better than bad sex.
- The myth that women who have had babies need larger dicks, is, for the most part...pretty true!

- If you're not going to have sex, you can at least use your hands and tongue.
- Guys like women to seduce them, but women **love** the same thing.
- Don't give up before you get started.
- Wounded women or going through PMS need sex MORE often; not less. They're lying to you if they say different.
- If a woman's giving you the cold shoulder and not talking to you, just seduce her. It will pretty much resolve everything.
- Women who are mom's do need a girl's night out, but more importantly, they need a babysitter to take the kids, and for YOU to take control of their bodies; not for minutes; but for HOURS!!!!
- I love going out to eat at good restaurants and I love to party; when I can find the right crowd (that's what Tantra Communities are for)!
- I used to work at a Gentleman's Club and loved it (as the massage girl)!
- Most people are sexually repressed and have one area or another of Sexual Wounding to heal, but most people think that they don't need to heal, when in fact you can ALWAYS expand yourself to another level, and it gets to the point of being VERY fun!
- I'd rather be honest than keep everything inside. The more honest you can be, the more in touch with your power you are, and the more passionate you become.
- Life is meant to be fun, but sometimes it takes a little work!
- Everyone is precious and deserves a chance!
- Sex can heal anything, and Tantra practices that is.

Asttarte Deva Shakti Bliss

**Section 9
Poetry**

Asttarte Deva Shakti Bliss

Radiating everywhere, a poem by Asttarte Deva

I surrender to the violet plane
I surrender to this body
I surrender to this mind
I breathe and let life in
I breathe and let fate take me
I am wholeness in peace
No one can take me back
but my own my ego,
my temptations,
my resistance
I am always in control
I let go and allow
as I am continuously filled with love.

Asttarte Deva Shakti Bliss

Just Allow, a poem by Asttarte Deva

People are always worried about things having to be something different than they are

They want things to be perfect

And their lack of patience overcomes them,

By their sense of impulsiveness towards perfection.

Time is not important in matters of the heart

Things always work out as God intended them to.

Trusting in the infinite comes to a deeper knowledge from accepting what is

Perfect is not perfect

It is accepting the perfection that things are already perfect

There's no need to rush

Or worry what is not

Things just are

And they come in the right time

The answers come

The desires come

Everything comes in perfect timing

Because it already is perfect just as it is

Things are love

Questioning love is questioning the self and God

Have no doubt

Be patient in yourself

Find the love within you to trust this patience

And all will be fine and at peace

There is no hurry

Just allow

Just Allow, 10-19-04, 6:43am

In response to:

"to love perfection is to hate life"

Asttarte Sharananda Deva

Pleasure With All Your Clothes On, a poem by Asttarte Deva

Empower yourself
Awaken Your Body
Awaken Your Mind
With your Breath
Your Breath Alone
Your Breath
Breathe, into stillness
Breathe into bliss
Breathe into your pain
Breathe into yourself
And watch, notice, feel
All of your sensations heightened
Feel all of you
Awake
Excitement of your senses
Be in touch with spirit
Let your spirit be touched
Your breath is the miracle to your healing
Your breath is the miracle to your pain
Your breath is the miracle to your pleasure
Full body, standing alone, all your clothes on kind of pleasure
Just stand and watch yourself be ignited with pleasure
As you breathe into your own ecstasy of the divine......
SO simple
Yet, so profound.

With Love, Asttarte

Asttarte Deva Shakti Bliss

Relationship Manifestation

When I view him as loving, he becomes loving
When I view him as timid, he becomes afraid
When I view him as angry, he gets angrier
When I view him as lazy, he becomes lazier and does nothing
When I view him as weak, he becomes fragile
When I view him as rageful, he becomes violent
When I view him as gentle, my heart melts, and he melts too
When I view him as innocent, he surrenders, and understands
When I view him as giving, he does everything in his power, with even as little as a tiny gift, and gives
When I view him as kind, he becomes kinder
When I view him as a teacher, I trust, and listen
When I view him as a Healer, I surrender and let him heal me
When I view him as loving, my hearts breaks down its wall, and becomes open.
Whatever I see in him, he becomes that exact thing.
He is my mirror, my self, the thing I most fear, or the thing I most love.
HE is the One, and all that is.

Asttarte Deva Shakti Bliss

Being Present

The moments of being in emptiness,
in the moment,
unaware of where you are or
what's going on around you,
are the moments when we are
most focused on what we're doing.
There is no thinking except
to what's in front of you,
next to you, and how you feel
inwardly. Judgments not are
made on anything in the world
The only thing that matters is
the intricate details of the thoughts
and flow of the moment. Minute factors
beyond this do not exist.

Asttarte Deva Shakti Bliss

The Love of A Stranger, a poem, by Asttarte Deva

When engaging in moments of an embrace in a strangers arms
Acceptance and unconditional love are met instantly
Like the euphoria of falling in love with a new lover
An encounter with the divine is welcomed in open arms of a stranger
With the breath, the presence,
And the openness to experience intimacy for what it is
Without a history of times past as in a deep-committed relationship
There are no triggers, no reminders of past hurts
The love of a stranger is met with openness
For no longing or hunger of a committed partner is there
One can just be,
And allow urges and awakenings to move gracefully
Across the air as a feather of a swift breath to the unknown
A stranger in the presence of the divine,
Can allow sudden passions to be awakened
Past memories or pains to be surrendered to this moment
In accepting what is, what feelings come up,
All memories or thoughts in the mind
That occurred before this moment
disappear
And everything become peaceful and beautiful once again
During these times we can forgive our present lovers
Or past lovers who we no longer share our lives with
We can just be, in love, with this new stranger
For a brief moment of time

Asttarte Deva Shakti Bliss

Vulnerability into Pleasure

Many people think tantra is just a term and an excuse to be sexual and erotic.
That is the furthest from the truth of what tantra truly is.
The purpose of tantra is not to be erotic
But to be loved.
How is tantra a path to feel love, but not feel erotic?
The answer is, it's both.
Safety and love must come before feeling sexual, period.
If someone tries to feel erotic before feeling safe and love,
they're skipping too many steps ahead.
Go back a few steps, and you might end up where you want to be.
Maybe you don't need to feel safe.
Maybe you don't have a single bone of softness in you.
Maybe you can jump into the sexual, before the sensual.
There is a layer of vulnerability there, you are unwilling to see.
Consider every human has fragile emotions.
You might just be covering yours up with erotic energy.
Slow down a little bit, and you'll feel love energy.
Give your partner a chance to catch up to your sexual energy,
and you'll both be a match
And intimate love will never be the same.
Do you feel anxious, irritable or frustrated?
What is it you are not letting yourself feel?
What are the feelings that are hiding underneath the surface?
What emotions are you hiding from?
What feelings popped up in a moment, and then went away soon after?
The pop-up feelings are a clue. Dig deeper.
Surrender to them. Breathe into them. Feel them.
Notice. Investigate. Become a detective to your own feelings.
Is it anger? Breathe into anger.
Is it sadness? Breathe into sadness.
It is regret? Breathe into regret.

Is it despair? Breathe into despair.
Is it joy? Breathe into joy.
Is it love? Breathe into love.
Any feeling you feel, and breathe into, will make the feeling bigger, and either move through your body and let go, or feel more love, more joy, and more pleasure as you breathe into them. Breathing into anger, despair, regret, sadness is loving them, and they will surrender, breathe through you, drop into nothingness, and transform into pleasure.
Tantra is a path of healing.
What is it you are healing today?
What parts of yourself are you expanding?
How will you shift vulnerability into pleasure today?
No one is ever going to be the same energy level at exactly the same time every time you desire it.
Someone is going to have to slow down and be patient for the other.
It's never about forcing someone to meet you where you are,
But always about surrendering to meet them where they are.
Are you surrendering to your Beloved?
Are you making them feel safe, or threatened?
Are you putting frustration onto them, or love?
Can you go deeper into surrender with yourself?
With your lover?
It just might turn your frustration into bliss.
Don't forget to breathe.
The breath is the key!
It is your vehicle. Your teacher. Your friend. Your lover.
Your life-force. Your heart. A connection to your soul
Something SO much bigger than you.
It is your gift!
And you have it with you all the time.

Note: Read this again after meditating, and it will make more sense!

Detachment, Surrender, Acceptance

Whoever forces it spoils it.
Whoever grasps it loses it.

-- Lao Tzu
The Art & Practice of Loving

Give up, and you will succeed.
Bow, and you will stand tall.
Be empty, and you will be filled.
Let go of the old, and let in the new.
Have little, and there is room to receive more.

The wise stand out,
because they see themselves as part of the Whole.
They shine,
because they don't want to impress.
They achieve great things,
because they don't look for recognition.
Their wisdom is contained in what they are,
not their opinions.
They refuse to argue,
So, no one argues with them.

The Ancients said: "Give up and you will succeed."
Is this empty nonsense?
Try it.
If you are sincere, you will find fulfillment.

Asttarte Deva Shakti Bliss

Spiritual Poetry on Love

Tao Te Ching, by: Stephen Mitchell
(From a beautiful Goddess friend's book named Emily Nussdorfer- Dance & Movement Arts Therapist. In our conversation, she had told me this is who I am, and I thanked her, and copied the poem.)

The Master has no mind of her own.
She works with the mind of the people.

She is good to people who are good.
She is also good to people who aren't good.
This is true goodness.

She trusts people who are trustworthy.
She also trusts people who aren't trustworthy.
This is true trust.

The Master's mind is like space.
People don't understand her.
They look to her and wait.
She treats them like her own children.

~~~~~~~~~~~~~~~

Excerpts from the poetry of Mevlâna Jalâluddîn Rumi **Versions by Coleman Barks From <u>Unseen Rain</u>**

Quatrains
Don't let your throat tighten with fear. Take sips of breath all day and night. Before death closes your mouth. There's no love in me without your being, no breath without that. I once thought   I could give up this longing, then thought again, *But I couldn't*

continue being human.

Excerpts from Love is a Stranger Poetry of Mevlâna Jalâluddîn Rumi Translated by Kabir Helminski

The Intellectual

The intellectual is always showing off;
The lover is always getting lost.
The intellectual runs away, afraid of drowning;
the whole business of love is to drown in the sea.
Intellectuals plan their repose;
lovers are ashamed to rest.
The lover is always alone, even surrounded with people;
like water and oil, he remains apart.
The man who goes to the trouble
of giving advice to a lover
gets nothing. He's mocked by passion.
Love is like musk. It attracts attention.
Love is a tree, and lovers are its shade.

Servant of Peace – Prayer of St Francis

Lord, make me an instrument of Thy peace;
where there is hatred, let me sow love;
where there is injury, pardon;
where there is doubt, faith;
where there is despair, hope;
where there is darkness, light;
where there is sadness, joy;
O Divine Master,
grant that I may not so much seek to be consoled as to console;
to be understood, as to understand;
to be loved, as to love;
for it is in giving that we receive,
it is in pardoning that we are pardoned,
and it is in dying that we are born into Eternal Life.

Asttarte Deva Shakti Bliss

**Section 10
Testimonials**

"I was engulfed...by your sensuality.
You treated me as though I was all that mattered to you and time slowed to a near halt to witness. Dealing with my apprehension and fears, you have made me face and overcome many of them. I dare not graduate to conquering all of them; because, I want you around for a long time.
Please continue to sharpen your sensitivity, fulfill your focus and sensationalize your sexuality and the sky will open to unlimited opportunities and vivid dreams. I only ask one thing of you during your rise: Take me with you."
regular client, 4/28/06

~~~~~~~~~~~~~~~~~~~~~~~~~~~

Asttarté

As you know I've been doing chakra meditation on my own for several months now. The idea was to harness the Kundalini energy to help me physically and mentally. I've been visualizing the chakras by color and location, and thinking about relaxing and releasing the energy from each while I chant the appropriate mantra. It took a few sessions, but I was surprised to feel anything at all, but I did. I started to feel a faint buzzing warmth in the first three chakras.

It took me about 2 months before I could feel anything at all beyond that.

I finally felt something in my heart, and soon after that in my brow (Unfortunately as a headache!). But I was getting in touch to a small degree with all my chakras.

Your session blew me away. By sharing your energy with me while I did a similar chakra meditation, it was a 100-fold more powerful. You were somehow able to help me release /and give to me/ energy in such a way it was overwhelming. I could feel stress, pain and tension flowing from me. I could feel a strong charge of energy. A few times it was almost too much it was such a heady experience. It was blissfully intoxicating. I also don't think I've ever felt that close to someone. It was such a close, intimate experience. For the first time I think I felt really "in tune" with another human being. That in itself was a pretty wonderful experience.

The down side of this is that I am now back to my own chakra meditation - by myself. It's a pale and poor substitute to what we shared. I feel like a junkie who got really high but now can't get another fix. My loneliness is intensified, after sharing that oneness, and then going back to being by myself.

Still - this gave me a small glimpse of how things could be, and how powerful this work is. It is something to look forward to, to continue to learn about, and hopefully get more adept at so I can harness these energies better own my own.
In summary, all I can say is "WOW, Let's do it again!"
Love and thankfulness,
Regular client, 4/10/06

...real treasure and treat!
Asttarté Sharananda Deva, Dakini:
Greetings! I trust that all is well with you.
Although I did leave a voicemail, I wanted to send this e-mail to you.

First, let me thank you for "fitting" me in today. I know that it was not scheduled until literally the last minute at a late hour. I felt that I should at least attempt to see you before this demanding day and weekend. I was oh so right. I really was out of balance and out of sync with myself for a couple of weeks now. I knew of no one to help me. My prior experiences weren't worth repeating and my possibilities were very slim. I could find a therapeutic massage that left something out and a sensual that was empty and frustrating. When you met me at the door I was relieved and felt that I was going to be correct about trusting you.

Second, let me thank you for a wonderful session. You advised me to "melt" and I melted before you advised me. Great touch, reading, rhythm and sensual strokes. I was very relaxed especially considering that the cats did not distract me. I felt peaceful and safe in my very vulnerable state. Your attention to my needs made me feel that no one else and nothing else mattered to you during the time we were together. I also appreciate your level of respect to me in not taking me too far too soon. I really admired that.

Third, since the session, I have traveled from Chester, West Chester and back to Delaware County. Mostly in the rain and in moderate to high volume traffic. Normally, I would be a nervous wreck. Because of you, not once did I get close to being "bent out of shape". I felt appreciated, balanced, confident, relaxed and (a hint) of sensual. All thanks to you and your work.

Fourth, if you allow, I would like to make another appointment with you. I will be away much of this week. If you would, please advise me of what you feel, based on this appointment today, of what I would be ready for? I mentioned tantric and you also confirmed that as a stage. Just wanted to get a feel of what you were feeling.

Fifth, I am very grateful to have met you. I have longed for an experience that awakens what was sleep or even untouched. I feel that you could remedy my need for chemistry, communication, expression, sensuality and sexuality in dosages that would be captivating and mutual without guilt, maintenance or obligation. I really appreciate your finding that and even more in me and being trustworthy to not mistreat it. I find that I would give if you receive my transparency, trust and vulnerability.

Finally, I apologize for the length. Some things can't be said in short sentences, small paragraphs and snappy dissertations. Sweet dreams and success for the days ahead.
New client, 4/9/06

Dear Asttarte'
Warm regards!
Please accept my sincere thanks for yesterday's session, together. It was such an awesome experience, and I thank you for your energy, love, and sacred healing. I feel renewed in heart, mind, and spirit.
Namaste!
T., client

Dear Asttarte,
I am still drinking in the generosity of spirit & soul you shared with me in our session. The way you touch, speak, breath & move is imbued with such a level of mastery that my sense of gratitude grew from your first words. Even though you used different modalities, you have woven them into a beautiful tapestry which is your work, your presence. Thank you again for being a teacher, a healer & most importantly being true to yourself.
Much Peace & Love,
Felipe

Asttarte Deva Shakti Bliss

"A devotee of your enchantment
and perfect religion summing up my heart
a worshiper of your perfect form
obedient love slave to your gorgeous goddess feet
my loving open mouth and servant tongue
shall obey the hints of your guiding feet
to please you anywhere in any way accepting all
Michael a fellow believer in the truth of love without shame as
a sacred right beyond the laws of possessiveness your man-
friend your woman-friend your artist-friend as well as faithful
regular client.
Michael who is smitten but not blind in the least
Michael who loves to recognize others
and be recognized."
Michael, Writer, Editor and Client.

"I have been blessed to know and work with Asttarte for several years. She is a woman of wisdom, compassion, love and a deeply Spiritual Being. Astarte brings to her healing and teaching a freshness and joy; a wealth of experience, a caring for all people and the inner desire to help, to heal and to give of all that she is and that is love."
Jim Curley, Director of One...A Shared Journey, Spiritual Life Coach.

"Asttarte is a gifted healer whose commitment to truth as a seeker and practitioner brings forth limitless possibilities in her work. Her selfless attitude of compassion and patience combined with the intensity of her belief in wellness as our natural state makes her a very effective vessel for God's Grace to heal others through her."

Love,
David Newman, Founder and Director of Yoga on Main, Manayunk, PA, and author, writer and singer.

"Asttarte is a wonderful healer who has a wealth of knowledge in many traditions. She is a very loving person with an open heart who personally cares for her patients and clients and treats them in body, mind, and Soul."
Swami Ramananda, President of New Life Yoga International, author of BLISS NOW and "Wings of the Dawn" CD.

"Asttarte Sharananda Deva is truly a gifted healer who masterfully balances her heart and intuition with her deep wisdom and expertise. Her session has enabled my husband and I to release discomfort and pain easily and effortlessly and have left us feeling deeply peaceful and recharged."

Rev. Andrea Miranda Thomas, RsCP, Spiritual Counselor, Workshop Facilitator

I went to see Asttarte last week; to heal my heart over upsetting text messages with a male friend. As I started to talk I ended up not just healing my heart of the pain of that message, but ended up healing my inner child!!!! The inner child of my twenties to now. was healed. I only one other time came close to healing the child of my past. It was almost four years ago. And was in a hospital and outpatient Setting. When I tried to accomplish the same thing with my therapist something was missing. I would say let's try this or that. But we never did, so I tried hypnosis. This has helped a little, but the work we did last week was like combining two weeks in the hospital, with two weeks outpatient, and hypnosis all in one (if this makes sense). I talked about things So deeply personal and painful. However, the whole time threw my tears I felt safe, understood, and not judged!!!! but loved in the sense "you Matter" I use my experience to keep me going. The little girl I call Joy is a work in progress. She isn't at the finish line, but she isn't at the beginning Or stuck anymore. She has friends to help her now!!!! Thank you Asttarte, HM, 2-3-14

... Your loving nurturing presence was the thing that supported me without fail in my process. Connecting to the breath was important. I fell in love with the sound of silence and my own breath. I felt like I was in a meditation most of the time. I was beginning to identify less and less with my thoughts.

... When I started listening to Dolano's open Satsang, I saw the ring of truth in everything she said, except I felt a little scared when she said there was nobody. After 3 weeks of listening to Dolano's satsang, there was an incident of calamity and chaos at work. I could feel the fear and panic overwhelmingly. I let the emotions move freely and after about 10 min a feeling of bliss began to build til I was filled with amazing joy in the middle of catastrophe! In this happening, I saw through the illusion of thought and came to know my true nature. All the dysfunctional stories I had built around sex and relationship dropped because there was no longer any body to suffer. I felt utterly loved and cared for. I realized, at my core essence, I had always been OK! I was free at last!

... Mind may still want to spin a good story. But now thoughts are seen as passing clouds, moving freely, a part of a greater whole, nothing to get worked up about.
...Your love and support were essential on my path of learning what is true! I am so grateful for your kindness!!!
MR, 2/2/14

Asttarte,
...Your power is like a surgeon's - it can heal, or with the subtlest slip of the wrist, it can also cut where not intended. It seems to me your healing, and your gift of giving yourself, giving healing, giving comfort, giving pleasure, make positive change possible by shining a light that the client can use as a lamp to do what is ultimately his/her own work, although facilitated by you as a catalyst.

   Your specialized knowledge and understanding are deep, your training extensive, your self-realization and obvious effort at

pursuing a spiritual path is inspiring, and your generous and unselfish willingness to impart to others - already obvious to me - is immense and unusual. Your penetrating intuition, empathy, as well as expressiveness and feeling are comforting, reassuring, affirming, and nothing short of a gift I already cherish.
D."

"Asttarte,
Thank you for a wonderful session this past Saturday. Your session helped me a lot, and I am grateful for the time you spent with me. It really helped me a lot, and gave me a connection with myself that I had lost for a long time. I would definitely continue my sessions with you.

Respectfully,
J."

"Asttarte, Again, thank you for your loving trust and honor you gave me last our last session. I never felt so understood in my feelings about how I wanted to make a woman feel loved as a person and not just a sex object. You are very good at what you teach.
Respect & Love!
H"

"Asttarte:
My visit with you earlier this week was amazing! Your spirituality and sensuality are what I would consider gifts...You have a healing power that I would not have believed if I personally did not experience it. I enjoyed every moment of your healing and felt rejuvenated and changed after two hours in your presence. I plan to continue to see you each time I am in the Philadelphia area and look forward to more spiritual growth."
JMB

"Hi Asttarte,
Just wanted to thank you again for our time together. I did feel all the stress leave my body and I will continue trying the breathing technique you showed me. I do wish we could spend more time together. I wish you luck on your own journey.
Your friend always, J."

"Asttarte,
Just wanted to send you a message to let you know that through the years I have experimented with healing,
I have to say that my most memorable experience was with you. You are beautiful both inside and out and are a true professional. Have a great day and looking forward to seeing you again.
B.D. from Delaware"

"Asttarte,
... thinking of you and of your generosity
What I learned from the brief times that I spent with you is that I matter. That physiologically I am fine. But more than that I learned a few things that I will take forward with me. One of those things is about myself; about me being a sexual being. And that what I wanted deep down is to express it, feel it, and have my own enthusiasm for it be returned. That is the one thing I got from you. I hope that came across the way it was meant (as a compliment).
.... I did want you to know that being with you was one of the most

peaceful experiences ever."
Always,
Richard

"Warm regards!
Please accept my sincere thanks for yesterday's session, together. It was such an awesome experience, and I thank you for your energy, love, and sacred healing. I feel renewed in heart, mind, and spirit.
Namaste!"
- T., client

Asttarte is a very loving and caring teacher and I always feel awakened with her love after leaving one of her sessions.
Thank you Asttarte for being there for me.
John Romeo 2011.1.11

"Dear Asttarte,
Thank you so much for your time and for working with me. I continue to practice the breathing exercises on a daily basis. I found that you beautifully encompass and embody genuine compassion, authenticity and a high level of Integrity both as a practitioner of the healing arts and as a professional counselor.

May you continue to shine, radiate and channelize your beautiful healing energies towards helping and coaching people overcome limitations in body, mind or soul and awaken to living more passionate, joyful and vibrant lives.

Love and light. GN

Asttarte Deva Shakti Bliss

Remembering Rama!!!

One of my best friends passed away, 12/10/2011.

I am still in total shock of his passing. I found out on Thursday, Dec. 15th, 2011, in a text message. I was just waiting for him to get out of a **rehab center**. He was on his way to health, and he was embarrassed to have me see him the way he was and requested powerfully for me to not visit him. I now wish I didn't listen to him.

We spoke over the phone often throughout his entire journey to recovery and I feel as though the doctors who were treating him didn't really know how to treat him; they were unsure of what his real diagnosis was, and he was treated like a guinea pig. I remember talking to him about filing a complaint on food poisoning to the Health Department as this is what triggered the **start** of the illness. I may want to follow up on this for him.

This is very sad news for all of us who knew him. Who he was for me was someone who truly cared about humanity and people. He was one of the most kind and loving people I've ever known, and some of the kindness that would come out of him would completely blow me away. He honored, respected and appreciated me more than anyone I've ever known. In truth, he adored me, and it was a closeness I haven't had in a very long time. We were incredible friends and he looked up to me often to help him in his relationships. He was someone that always had a smile on his face, but deep down he was really sad and lonely. People appreciated him, respected him and looked up to him as a teacher. He was an incredible musician; a genius, and has been performing all over the world for the past decade. I just found out last night that his father who taught him everything he knew is a legend in **music** in India and in the United States and his compositions are all around the world. And my dear friend shared that knowledge with everyone he knew.

He performed in a band with David Newman and he would often come home from being on tour and spend some time with me. He would share with me the difficulties he had with his friend David, but my dear friend Rama never once judged him or made him wrong for who he was. He was incredibly loyal and devoted to the people in his life. He is known by many in the Yoga Communities, as well as some of those in Common Ground.

The past year and 1/2 he started teaching music to young children and a few of his **students** were at the memorial last night. I got to share with them what he meant to me in private and they shared with me what he meant to them. He was deeply loved, and he will be very very missed.

I will be in communication with his family and available to **support** them in their time of grieving. I know his father is impacted the most, and I feel more sad for him than anyone. Rama was supporting him in his own health and taking care of him. Now his father is at a treatment center and is being cared for by nurses. My heart is open to his whole family, and my heart has been blown open because of this. I will be grieving for perhaps some time as well.

May you all please pray to him. He is still here hanging around on the Earth realms and is easily available in Spirit when called upon. I know he trying to make sense of all of this as well!

I'm sorry to be writing this to you this late. There was a memorial service for him this past Friday, Dec. 16th at Jai Yoga Studio and on Saturday evening at Yoga on Main in Manayunk, PA. I was grieving deeply all weekend, so to those who are just getting this message, please know my heart is with you. If you wish to reach out to me, or want to connect to anyone who was impacted, feel free to let me know!

Much Love, Asttarte

About The Author

Asttarte Sharananda Deva Shakti Bliss, Intuitive, has been an Intuitive since birth, was Ordained as an Interfaith Minister Melchizedek Priestess in 2001, a Reiki Master Energy Healer since 1997, Massage Therapist (Shiatsu and Thai) and Acupressurist since 2001, and Yoga Teacher since 2005. She became Initiated as a Tantric Goddess Dakini in 2005, and a Mentor, Life, Sex and Relationship Coach in 2010.

Asttarte has a degree in Behavioral Science of Anthropology focused on World Religions, Psychology/ Sociology and English/Creative Writing in order to connect to all people from all cultures. She's been studying Holistic Healing and truly on the path to "find myself" since December of 1995 after being a part of a major Environmental Entrepreneurial company.

Published in the books:
The Mystery of Woman; a Book for Men
How to Make Sacred Love to a Woman: An Intimate Exploration of Sacred Sexuality, by Gabriel Morris
Recovering the Spirit; From Sexual Trauma; From the Traumatic to the Ecstatic, by Kylie Devi

She regularly teaches her style of Kundalini Orgasmic Meditation and is featured often as a presenter at Iron Garden in Newark, NJ right outside of NYC.

Asttarte helps one to find their true nature, unraveling the blocks to ultimate bliss, opening their heart, and cleansing the energetic, emotional and sexual blocks in the way. Asttarte teaches people how to master their own energy and cultivates practices that will bring you fresh in mind, spirit and joy! Bliss and ecstasy will come naturally, and you will know your true potential.

Whatever you are dealing with, she will support you to help empower, inspire, heal, and awaken your joy and love for life again!

Asttarte can be found at AsttarteDeva.com, LoveSexandTea.com, And HealingSacredWoman.com

www.ingramcontent.com/pod-product-compliance
Lightning Source LLC
Chambersburg PA
CBHW050854160426
43194CB00011B/2149